Mírzá Mihdí

Mírzá Mihdí (1848–70)

I have, O my Lord, offered up that which Thou hast given Me, that Thy servants may be quickened and all that dwell on earth be united.

Bahá'u'lláh

Tablet of Bahá'u'lláh revealed on the day of the martyrdom of the Purest Branch

Its translation begins
'Lauded be Thy name, O Lord my God!'[1]

Tablet of Bahá'u'lláh revealed after the martyrdom of the Purest Branch at the time of washing the body of Mírzá Mihdí

Its translation includes the words
'At this very moment . . . My son is being washed before My face'[2]

Mírzá Mihdí
The Purest Branch

by

Boris Handal

George Ronald
Oxford

George Ronald, *Publisher*
Oxford
www.grbooks.com

© Boris Handal 2017
Reprinted 2021

All Rights Reserved

*A catalogue record for this book is available
from the British Library*

ISBN 978–0–85398–606–5

Cover photograph: Nathalie Sandra Bellato
Cover design: Rene Steiner, Steinergraphics.com

Contents

List of Illustrations viii
Acknowledgements xi
Foreword, by Moojan Momen xiii

1 'Akká, the Most Great Prison 1
2 The Purest Branch 10
3 Early Years in Tehran 19
4 Exile in Baghdad, Constantinople and Adrianople 32
5 The Long Journey to 'Akká 50
6 The Disembarkation in 'Akká 69
7 Life in the Barracks 81
8 The First Bahá'í Pilgrims 113
9 The Treasure of God in the Holy Land 139
10 The Great Redemptive Sacrifice of the Purest Branch 156
11 Life without Mírzá Mihdí 162
12 A Monument to the Purest Branch 176
13 The Ode of the Dove 183
14 Epilogue 194

Appendix The Burial of the Purest Branch and the
    Mother of 'Abdu'l-Bahá by Rúḥíyyih Rabbani 209

Bibliography 221
Notes and References 227
Index 239

List of Illustrations

Frontispiece
1 Mírzá Mihdí (1848–1870)
2 Tablet of Bahá'u'lláh revealed on the day of the martyrdom of the Purest Branch
3 Tablet of Bahá'u'lláh revealed after the martyrdom of the Purest Branch at the time of washing the body of Mírzá Mihdí

Between pages 36 and 37
5 Násiri'd-Dín Sháh of Iran (1848–96)
6 Sulṭán 'Abdu'l-Azíz of the Ottoman Empire (1830–76)
7 A view of Tehran in the time of Mírzá Mihdí
8 Historical view of Baghdad and the Tigris River
9 The bridge at Büyükçekmece, Turkey, over which Mírzá Mihdí crossed with his father Bahá'u'lláh, his family and their companions on their way from Constantinople to Adrianople in December 1863
10 One of the houses in which Mírzá Mihdí lived with Bahá'u'lláh and His family in Adrianople
11 A group of exiled Bahá'ís in Adrianople. Mírzá Mihdí and 'Abdu'l-Bahá are the second and third from the left
12 Detail from the picture above, showing Mírzá Mihdí, left, with his brother 'Abdu'l-Bahá, in Adrianople
13 Bahíyyih Khánum, The Greatest Holy Leaf, in Adrianople
14 *The Arciduca Ferdinando Massimiliano*, built in 1856, in which Mírzá Mihdí, Bahá'u'lláh and His family and companions may have travelled from Gallipoli to Haifa
15 *Passengers on the Deck of a Steam Packet in the Adriatic Sea* by Henry Burdon Richardson
16 The sea gate through which Mírzá Mihdí entered 'Akká with Bahá'u'lláh, the family and companions in 1868
17 A street in 'Akká, typical of those along which Mírzá Mihdí walked with Bahá'u'lláh and the exiles to the barracks
18 When they first arrived at the citadel, Bahá'u'lláh, Mírzá Mihdí and the other exiles were taken to rooms adjoining the barracks square
19 Layout of the prison
20 'Akká
21 The Citadel in 'Akká

Between pages 132 and 133

21 Entrance into the citadel, the Most Great Prison
22 The door on the left leads to Bahá'u'lláh's cell
23 Bahá'u'lláh's cell in the citadel
24 Bahá'u'lláh's cell, refurbished in 2004
25 The two windows on the far right on the top floor of the citadel are in the cell occupied by Bahá'u'lláh
26 The window in Bahá'u'lláh's cell through which He would extend His hand to greet the pilgrims unable to enter the citadel
27 View from the refurbished window today
28 Abu'l-Ḥasan-i-Ardikání (Ḥájí Amín), the first pilgrim to meet Bahá'u'lláh within 'Akká's walls
29 Badí', who, dressed as a water-carrier bearing the tools of his trade, was introduced into the barracks and attained Bahá'u'lláh's presence
30 The roof of the prison where Mírzá Mihdí walked
31 Photo map of northern section, city of 'Akká.
32 The skylight, refurbished, through which Mírzá Mihdí fell onto a wooden crate below
33 During the restoration of the prison it was decided to leave untouched the floor where Mírzá Mihdí fell. The stairs to the roof are in the background
34 The Nabí Ṣáliḥ cemetery on the outskirts of 'Akká where Mírzá Mihdí was first buried. His headstone is on the right
35 The Nabí Ṣáliḥ cemetery in 2017. Note the space where the grave of Mírzá Mihdí originally stood
36 The original headstone over Mírzá Mihdí's grave at the Nabí Ṣáliḥ cemetery
37 The House of 'Abbúd, one of the houses in which Bahá'u'lláh and His family lived after they left the citadel. Navváb passed away in this house

Between pages 180 and 181

38 The monument marking the resting place of the Greatest Holy Leaf, circa 1932
39 The monument over the grave of the Greatest Holy Leaf
40 and 41 Monuments to Mírzá Mihdí and Navváb
42 Bronze plaque on the monument to Mírzá Mihdí
43 Monuments to Mírzá Mihdí and Navváb
44 and 45 Today, Bahá'í youth all over the world, inspired by the service and sacrifice of the Purest Branch, are studying the teachings of Bahá'u'lláh, building their capacity and arising in sacrificial service to their communities

To
Mas'úd Khamsí
for being an excellent role model in my life

Acknowledgements

With my heart overflowing with undying love and ineffable appreciation for the Universal House of Justice, I would like to express my gratitude for its unfailing guidance and encouragement, which has advanced the book through its various milestones. Additionally, my humble gratitude is directed towards the Research Department of the Baháʼí World Centre for sharing invaluable historical information which imbued the narrative with a fresh measure of spirit. With this in mind, I would like to also acknowledge the Audio-Visual Department of the Baháʼí World Centre for providing permission to reproduce many of the photographs which will, no doubt, leave indelible impressions and treasured memories in the hearts and minds of countless generations.

In like manner, I am moved to extend my heartfelt gratitude to Dr Felicity Rawlings-Sanaei, Melanie Price, Nur Mihrshahi and Dr Adren Alinejad for their valuable editorial contributions. Similarly, there are no befitting words to illustrate my profound appreciation for the outstanding and expert contributions of Dr Wendi Momen in bringing this book to life.

Additionally, my profound and sincere thanks to Dr Moojan Momen for his uplifting and peerless Foreword to the book, highlighting in inspiring and motivating terms the unparalleled sacrifices of the beloved and deeply cherished Mírzá Mihdí.

I also would like to kindly thank Mr Greg Page-Turner from Artware Fine Art (www.artwarefineart.com) for giving permission to use the image of the painting *Passengers on the Deck of a Steam Packet in the Adriatic Sea* by Henry Burdon Richardson. Similarly, my utmost appreciation to Mr Nury Eady for allowing the reproduction of his photograph of the roof of the 'Akká barracks.

Finally, to the two people in my life who hold a warm and abiding place in my tender heart, who are dearest and nearest, who are a constant source of inspiring joy and motivating encouragement and who through their unconditional love, support and affection have safeguarded me from ever feeling disheartened and discouraged. My dearest wife, Parvin, and daughter, Camelia, thank you for not only being helpful research assistants, but also for your perpetual positivity and encouragement ensuring that the final manuscript engages and uplifts the reader.

Boris Handal
Sydney, Australia
February 2017

Foreword

In the epilogue to his survey of the events of the first one hundred years of the Bahá'í Faith, Shoghi Effendi points out that the history of this religion has not proceeded smoothly in an ever-upward path. Rather it 'may be said to resolve itself into a series of pulsations, of alternating crises and triumphs, leading it ever nearer to its divinely appointed destiny'.[1] The crises that have descended upon the religion of Bahá'u'lláh have been, in Shoghi Effendi's estimation 'such as to exceed in gravity those from which the religions of the past have suffered'.[2] But in a mysterious spiritual alchemy, each act of sacrifice that is at the heart of the crises that affect the Bahá'í Faith generates the spiritual impulse that enables the subsequent victory to occur.

Although we will never fully understand the workings of these hidden spiritual processes, they operate just as surely as the laws of science. Shoghi Effendi has delineated so many instances of this phenomenon of alternating crises and victories in the history of the Bahá'í Faith[3] that we can be sure of the potency and effectiveness of this mechanism. In one analogy its working has been likened to a seed that must first sacrifice itself and be annihilated in order for the seedling to sprout from it and eventually become a mighty oak. In another metaphor it is likened to the crushing of seeds in a mill which is required to yield the oil which can then be put in a lamp and lit to cast the light that can illumine all. Only the act of sacrifice carried out with purity and sincerity can galvanize the spiritual energy that overcomes all obstacles and propels the religion forward to the next stage of its development.

It is in the nature of the mystery of sacrifice that those who sacrifice themselves are often not aware of, or underestimate, the full extent of the spiritual power they are unlocking. And this seems to have been the case with the act of sacrifice that forms the heart of the subject matter of this book. When Mírzá Mihdí, the Purest Branch, fell from a skylight one day in 1870 in 'Akká, he was severely injured and everyone could see that he was likely to die from his injuries. He was offered his life by his father Bahá'u'lláh. Mírzá Mihdí chose, however, to sacrifice his life, saying that he hoped that it would result in the gates of the prison being opened such that the Bahá'ís could visit Bahá'u'lláh once more. His sacrifice was accepted by Bahá'u'lláh and a few months after Mírzá Mihdí's death, the gates of the prison were indeed opened and Bahá'u'lláh moved to a house where the Bahá'í pilgrims could visit Him.

This was not, however, to be the only result of the sacrifice made by one who was the Purest Branch. This sacrifice was raised by Bahá'u'lláh to the same station as the great sacrifices of humanity's religious history, 'to the rank of those great acts of atonement associated with Abraham's intended sacrifice of His son, with the crucifixion of Jesus Christ and the martyrdom of the Imám Ḥusayn'.[4] Mírzá Mihdí's act of sacrifice unleashed the spiritual energies needed to achieve the ultimate aim of Bahá'u'lláh's revelation – to bring about the spiritual regeneration of the individual and the unity of the people of the world: 'Say: This Youth hath come to quicken the world and unite all its peoples.'[5] And the spiritual power to enable this to occur was unleashed through Mírzá Mihdí's act of sacrifice: 'I have, O my Lord, offered up that which Thou hast given Me, that Thy servants may be quickened and all that dwell on earth be united.'[6]

Of course, this aim of the spiritual regeneration of individual human beings and uniting the peoples of the world has not occurred yet and so the spiritual energies released by the sacrifice of Mírzá Mihdí's act of sacrifice are still at work today, inspiring individual Bahá'ís to acts of sacrifice to bring this about and driving the process forward.

Moojan Momen
Northill
February 2017

1

'Akká, the Most Great Prison

In biblical times there was a seaside city known by the Greeks and Romans as Ptolemais and by the ancient Egyptians as 'Akká. Over the centuries the city had been known by different names. In Old Testament times it was known as Accho[1] and Achor,[2] while it was renamed St Jean d'Acre (Acre) by the crusaders. The Muslims restored the name 'Akká.

Scholars reckon 'Akká to have existed for four thousand years. Muhammad is reported to have emphasized the spiritual station of the city: 'Blessed the man that hath visited 'Akká, and blessed he that hath visited the visitor of 'Akká.'[3]

'Akká is located in the Holy Land, now the state of Israel, in the vicinity of Mount Carmel, on the shores of one of the most beautiful bays of the Mediterranean Sea, some 175 kilometres north of Jerusalem. 'Akká was the scene of cruel clashes between Muslims and Christians during the Crusades, with the victorious Crusaders establishing it as the capital of the kingdom of Jerusalem. Napoleon and his powerful army laid siege to 'Akká but were incapable of taking the city after two months, leaving on its walls impressions of cannon balls and contemptuously calling it a 'grain of sand' for standing in the way of his military ambitions.[4] 'Akká was also referred to as the 'Turkish Bastille'.[5]

The tongues of the prophets of Israel had acclaimed the city, conferring upon it a special position in the course of human history. Indeed, 'Akká had been alluded to as the 'fortified' or 'strong' city,[6] a 'door of hope',[7] and where the 'Lord of Hosts', the 'King of Glory', would appear.[8]

Twenty-eight centuries ago, Hosea said:

> There I will give her back her vineyards, and will make the Valley of Achor a door of hope. There she will respond as in the days of her youth, as in the day she came up out of Egypt.[9]

David, the Psalmist, had also sung of the coming of Bahá'u'lláh to the 'Akká gates, 'Blessed be the Lord, for he hath shewn his wonderful mercy to me in a fortified city,'[10] asking, 'Who will lead me to the fortified city?'[11] He further proclaims:

> Lift up your heads, you gates;
> be lifted up, you ancient doors,
> that the King of glory may come in.
> Who is this King of glory?

> The Lord strong and mighty,
> the Lord mighty in battle.
> Lift up your heads, you gates;
> lift them up, you ancient doors,
> that the King of glory may come in.
> Who is he, this King of glory?
> The Lord Almighty –
> he is the King of glory.[12]

In turn, Ezekiel, one of the greatest and most prolific visionaries of the Jewish people, spoke of his wonderful mystical experiences:

> Then the man brought me to the gate facing east, and I saw the glory of the God of Israel coming from the east. His voice was like the roar of rushing waters, and the land was radiant with his glory . . . The glory of the Lord entered the temple through the gate facing east.[13]

Amos also announced the coming of Bahá'u'lláh to the Holy Land:

> The Lord will roar from Jerusalem; he will send his voice from Jerusalem. The pastures of the shepherds will become dry, and even the top of Mount Carmel will dry up.[14]

Over the years, this very blessed city experienced

several roles, being a town of merchants, the last Crusaders' stronghold, a fortress and later a prison-city at the time of the Ottoman Empire, when Bahá'u'lláh came 'through the gate facing the east' 'like the roar of rushing waters'.

It is with the arrival of Bahá'u'lláh, the Blessed Perfection, to those shores in 1868, that all these prophecies found a happy consummation, when finally He proclaimed that He Himself, the Lord of Hosts, the King of Glory, had appeared in the Holy Land. As God promised to humanity, 'In that day also he shall come even to thee from Assyria, and from the fortified cities, and from the fortress even to the river, and from sea to sea, and from mountain to mountain.'[15]

Bahá'u'lláh manifested His Cause in the Holy Land, the last destination of His successive exiles, following an edict from the Sultan of Turkey confining Him as well as the Holy Family to life imprisonment.

It was plainly evident, especially to the bereaved and remote Bahá'í community in Iran, the old Persia, that the enemies of the Faith had allied as never before to precipitate this severe blow. But above all else, it was clear that the Will and the Divine Plan were acting, and with the coming of the Supreme Manifestation of God to these sacred lands, all the prophecies were fulfilled.

The greatness of the Faith of Bahá'u'lláh then shone with maximum light while the peoples of the earth began to realize and wake up to this mighty Call. 'Abdu'l-Bahá said:

> When Bahá'u'lláh came to this prison in the Holy Land, the wise men realized that the glad tidings which God gave through the tongue of the Prophets two or three thousand years before were again manifested, and that God was faithful to His promise; for to some of the Prophets He had revealed and given the good news that 'the Lord of Hosts should be manifested in the Holy Land'. All these promises were fulfilled; and it is difficult to understand how Bahá'u'lláh could have been obliged to leave Persia, and to pitch His tent in this Holy Land, but for the persecution of His enemies, His banishment and exile. His enemies intended that His imprisonment should completely destroy and annihilate the blessed Cause, but this prison was in reality of the greatest assistance and became the means of its development. The divine renown of Bahá'u'lláh reached the East and the West, and the rays of the Sun of Truth illuminated all the world. Praise be to God! though He was a prisoner, His tent was raised on Mount Carmel, and He moved abroad with the greatest majesty. Every person, friend or stranger, who came into His presence used to say, 'This is a prince, not a captive.'[16]

The significance of the historic occasion, however, offered as the principle of light and shadow, exemplifies a marked contrast to the degradation of the character of the majority of the population, reflected in the customs and mentality of its authorities and the populace. Bahá'u'lláh described 'Akká's inhabitants as a 'generation of vipers'.[17]

In a way, the abject condition of these people was neither worse nor better than the material reality of the prison-city. The Sultan of Turkey, allied with the Shah of Iran, could not have found a more detestable place within his vast domain to imprison the Manifestation of God in order to extinguish the source of that Divine Light. The Blessed Perfection characterized 'Akká as 'the most desolate of the cities of the world, the most unsightly of them in appearance, the most detestable in climate, and the foulest in water. It is as though it were the metropolis of the owl.'[18]

A saying that was widely known stated that if a bird flew over the city, it would die from the pestilence. 'Akká housed the cruellest criminals, irremediable thieves, political prisoners and anybody else that the Sultan wanted to eliminate. The prison-city was framed within the irregular perimeter of a chain of walls washed on two sides by the sewage and the contaminated waters that waves swept inland to add more misery to the landscape.

The Guardian of the Bahá'í Faith, Shoghi Effendi, has commented about 'Akká's environment:

It was girt about by a double system of ramparts; was inhabited by a people whom Bahá'u'lláh stigmatized as 'the generation of vipers'; was devoid of any source of water within its gates; was flea-infested, damp and honey-combed with gloomy, filthy and tortuous lanes.[19]

The land gate was closed at night. It was called 'the dogs' door'[20] because after hours people had to pass through a narrow hole to enter or exit the city. To one side, facing the sea, stands the massive building known as the citadel, also called the barracks. It had been built during the 1790s on Crusader foundations as part of the Ottoman's defensive formation of 'Akká and housed army troops. In the 19th century it was converted into a gaol. The citadel looks like a small medieval castle standing adjacent to the Mediterranean Sea.

The entrance was through a spacious courtyard with a pool from which flea-infested and dirty water was drawn. On one side of the courtyard stood the prison block consisting of two floors. A narrow external staircase still leads to the roof, a place where better air could be breathed and one could view a beautiful landscape comprising the sea, the plains and the mountains.

Coming from Adrianople where He had lived in exile for five years, which has been preceded by a four-month sojourn in Constantinople and, before that, ten years' exile in Baghdad, Bahá'u'lláh arrived at the Most Great Prison by boat, crossing from Haifa to 'Akká's sea gate on 31 August 1868. Upon His arrival a crowd gathered at the port to see the 'God of the Persians', as they called Him, hurling invectives and the most cruel scorn. The group of 67 men, women and children were immediately taken inside the citadel and imprisoned in the barracks from the first night. Some days later the people rushed to the main mosque to hear the royal edict that ordered His strict detention and outlined the details of the rigour.

Within the walls of this stronghold the pain and suffering of the Holy Family reached its most intense agony, which lasted two years, two months and five days living in three small rooms. According to Bahíyyih Khánum, Bahá'u'lláh's daughter, she only left the building three times, and for only one hour, during the whole imprisonment.

Following Mírzá Mihdí's passing in June 1870, the exiles were moved to accommodate troops which required use of the barracks. The Blessed Beauty was required to live in a rented house outside the barracks. He lived in three houses before moving to the House of 'Abbúd within the prison-city, always as a prisoner.

Gradually, the conditions were relaxed owing to the growing public recognition of the good character of the exiles and the edict of the Sultan became virtually redundant. The character of the innocent group of exiles began to be appreciated by the local authorities, several of whom admired Bahá'u'lláh's special personality and stature, to the extent that the admiration of some, initially very hostile, was expressed in the assertion that such special people had never before been seen in 'Akká. They even speculated that the steady and positive transformation in 'Akká's climate was due to the presence of His Holiness Bahá'u'lláh.

The exiles were allowed to roam freely around the prison-city without escort. Bahá'u'lláh's confinement within the prison walls of 'Akká lasted nearly nine years, during which He 'had not set foot beyond the city walls, and Whose sole exercise had been to pace, in monotonous repetition, the floor of His bed-chamber'.[21]

Historical events took place in the Most Great Prison such as the revelation of the Kitáb-i-Aqdas, the Book of Laws; the addressing of epistles to the various kings and leaders of the world; as well as the formulation of a vast number of teachings for humanity. The Blessed Beauty said to 'Abdu'l-Bahá on His arrival in 'Akká, that henceforth He would dedicate all His time to formulating His teachings for the human race and meeting with His disciples while 'Abdu'l-Bahá's duty would be to deal with the outside world and the affairs of the Cause.[22]

'Know thou,' Bahá'u'lláh wrote, 'that upon Our arrival at this Spot, We chose to designate it as the "Most Great Prison". Though previously subjected in another land (Tihrán) to chains and fetters, We yet refused to call it by that name. Say: Ponder thereon, O ye endued with understanding!'[23]

2

The Purest Branch

Within the grey and cold walls of 'Akká entered Mírzá Mihdí, the young and pious son of Bahá'u'lláh. He was the third living child of the marriage of Bahá'u'lláh and Ásíyih Khánum, four years younger than 'Abdu'l-Bahá. The marriage produced at least seven children: Kázim, Ṣádiq, 'Abdu'l-Bahá, 'Alí-Muḥammad, Bahíyyih Khánum, Mírzá Mihdí and another child called 'Alí-Muḥammad. One source mentions the name of Mihdí instead of Ṣádiq. Only three children – 'Abdu'l-Bahá, Bahíyyih Khánum and Mírzá Mihdí – survived to adulthood. We also know that two of the children born before 'Abdu'l-Bahá, one about 1840 and the other about 1842, died in infancy.

Mírzá Mihdí was born Mihdí Núrí; Núrí means 'coming from Núr', Bahá'u'lláh's ancestral birthplace. Mírzá Mihdí saw the light of day sometime in 1848 in a house rented by the family near the Shimrán Gate, one of the main entrances to the city of Tehran. In that house, which still stands, Bahá'u'lláh lived with His extended family, including His wife, mother, brothers and sister, until His last days in Iran.

Mírzá Mihdí was named after Bahá'u'lláh's elder

brother, who was very much loved by Him and who had died about a year before Mírzá Mihdí's birth. Mírzá is a title and Mihdí is Arabic for 'rightly guided'.[1] He was born in 1848, a year of intense persecution against the followers of the Báb.

From his early years he had to suffer the weight of the tribulations of his father. For example, in 1852 Bahá'u'lláh was imprisoned in the infamous Síyáh-Chál of Tehran. As explained in the next chapter, the danger of His being executed at any time because He was a Bábí[2] was imminent. The family therefore had to hide and look every day for a channel that could tell them whether or not Bahá'u'lláh was still alive.

Later, when Bahá'u'lláh and His family left Iran for Baghdad as exiles in January 1853, Mírzá Mihdí was very small and had to remain in Tehran owing to illness and the vicissitudes of the very difficult trip in mid-winter. According to Bahíyyih Khánum, 'my mother allowed herself to be persuaded to leave the little fellow, only two years old, with her grandmother, though the parting with him was very sad.'[3]

In 1858 Mírzá Mihdí was brought to Baghdad by a member of the family living in the city who, apparently, was not on the list of exiles and was able to travel back to Iran. When Mírzá Mihdí returned to his family he was probably eleven years old and had missed out an important formative period of his life, away from parents' and siblings' direct care and affection. We do not have information about his life experiences during that period. However, we can imagine that after all those years of separation, the reunion must have brought immense happiness to the family at a time when the means of communication were very rudimentary and news did not come frequently. Having had his last contact with Bahá'u'lláh at the tender age of four years, it is fair to say that this was the first time he knew Him as his father.

There is not much information about Mírzá Mihdí's life between the ages of four and eleven when he was in the care of his maternal great-grandmother[4] and paternal aunt[5] while his parents were in Baghdad. Other authors maintain that he was left with his maternal grandmother[6] or 'relatives'.[7] We do not know whether his great-grandmother was a believer in the Báb and therefore able to guide him to the truths of the Cause of God. His paternal aunt, Bahá'u'lláh's sister Sárih Khánum, was, however, a devoted believer to whom the Blessed Beauty revealed many Tablets. She died in 1879 or 1880. It is possible to assume that Mírzá Mihdí, given the extended nature of Persian families, was engaged with many relatives of the same age. At an age when children need their parents the most, Mírzá Mihdí may have looked towards other family members for role models.

He probably had plenty of cousins to play with as well as uncles and aunts to look after him. Regardless of the religious attitudes of his Muslim relatives, Mírzá Mihdí must have enjoyed playing because children, as pure souls, are not prejudiced as some become as adults, just as Jesus Christ said, '. . . unless you change and become like little children, you will never enter the kingdom of heaven'.[8] As difficult as it is for a child to have memories before the age of four, equally complex is it to keep imagining for seven years what your parents and siblings might look like and thinking of them every night once total silence wraps you in your bed. Mírzá Mihdí may have thought about his parents and siblings, and may have wondered what it would be like to hug them, to eat dinner with them, to play with his brother and sister as they had played together in earlier days.

Baghdad and Tehran were among the major cities in Asia at the time of Bahá'u'lláh. Both were honoured by Him with elevated spiritual titles. While the first was characterized as the 'Abode of Peace',[9] the latter was called 'Mother of the World'.[10] The distance between the cities is about 900 km, which nowadays takes about 75 minutes to fly across. However, in earlier times people travelled together in carriages, on horseback, walking and in caravans because of the long trip and the danger of thieves along the roads. This was a route that had been travelled for centuries, even millennia, a part of the legendary Silk Road that linked the cities of antiquity, bringing together cultures and promoting trade. We know that when Bahá'u'lláh and His family were exiled from Tehran and travelled to Baghdad during the snowy winter of early 1853 the journey took three months.

After seven years the time came for Mírzá Mihdí to be brought to his parents. Entering foreign territories, where languages other than Farsi – such as Kurdish and Arabic – were spoken and people dressed in different costumes must have been a special experience for the young Mírzá Mihdí. At that time not many people crossed the frontiers of their own country owing to poor transportation and lack of facilities. Hence, for our youth such a trip must have been an event much anticipated. It required stopping at various places along the road in lodges called caravanserais which were located throughout a vast territory populated by isolated villages and nomadic tribes. On the serpentine route the traveller wandered through deserts, valleys, plateaus, by waterfalls and across the high Zagros Mountains and finally reached Baghdad, situated on the banks of the river Tigris. Mírzá Mihdí had arrived at his long-awaited home, where all troubles of the past finally had ended because he was now in his parents' arms.

We do not know how much exposure he had to the faith of his parents but it is certainly true that Mírzá Mihdí began to flourish upon his arrival in Baghdad. And he did well because a few years later he had become

Bahá'u'lláh's personal and efficient amanuensis. Being an amanuensis was not only a qualified job but one given as a spiritual privilege to selected believers.

By then, Bahá'u'lláh had already returned from a two-year spiritual withdrawal to the mountains of Sulaymáníyyih. We also know that Mírzá Mihdí, then aged 14, was present in the Garden of Riḍván during the days when Bahá'u'lláh declared His prophetic mission in April–May 1863. For successive years he shared firsthand the bitter pain which was always present in Bahá'u'lláh's exile and imprisonment, first to Constantinople for four months and later to Adrianople for nearly five years.

Mírzá Mihdí never attended school as the fragmentation of his life would not allow it. It is said that he received lessons from his mother who was literate, unlike the majority of women in those years. Despite his lack of schooling, he grew in wisdom and in the cultivation of spiritual qualities. For his soul's nobility the Blessed Perfection conferred upon him the title of 'The Purest Branch' (Ghuṣn-i-Aṭhar). In this metaphor, Bahá'u'lláh represents the Tree of Life, His male relatives were referred to as Branches while women were Leaves of that blessed Tree. For example, 'Abdu'l-Bahá is the Most Great Branch and Bahíyyih Khánum is the Greatest Holy Leaf.

It has been said that Mírzá Mihdí was very similar to 'Abdu'l-Bahá, though a little taller and thinner. They had great affection for each other. An early believer described Mírzá Mihdí as 'truly the brother of 'Abdu'l-Bahá, extremely modest and self-effacing'.[11] He was also described as 'endowed with a character of superlative spiritual beauty'.[12]

Hasan M. Balyuzi, distinguished historian, wrote of Mírzá Mihdí:

> According to Áqá Riḍá's testimony, who had seen him [Mírzá Mihdí] grow up to young manhood, he was a pillar of strength amongst the companions, from the days they came out of Baghdád to the day a tragic mishap brought his short and unsullied life to its conclusion, sitting with them at their gatherings, reading to them of that which flowed from the Supreme Pen, teaching them the lessons of courtesy and patience, of dignity and radiant submission to the will of God.[13]

Another companion of the barracks describes him in the following terms:

> It is not possible for anyone to visualize the measure of humility and self-effacement and the intensity of devotion and meekness which the Purest Branch evinced in his life.[14]

Owing to Mírzá Mihdí's excellent calligraphy, an art highly prized at that time, he became an amanuensis to his father in Adrianople, becoming proficient in this skill. In that city he devoted himself to transcribing the sacred Tablets, which are still extant in his handwriting. After his daily work, he met with the Bahá'ís and shared with them the newly revealed verses. He was also a comfort to the friends, encouraging them to endure with patience the rigours of exile and imprisonment.

As mentioned earlier, the order of Sultan 'Abdu'l-'Azíz was that the entire group of exiles along with Bahá'u'lláh were to be transferred to the stronghold of the prison-city of 'Akká. The sentence of life imprisonment without reprieve was highly restrictive and harsh, and did not allow the prisoners to associate with the local population, forcing them into maximum isolation. The desolation of the city, its scorching heat, foul air and unbearable conditions, can be better appreciated through the words of the Divine Messenger:

> 'None knoweth what befell Us, except God, the Almighty, the All-Knowing . . . From the foundation of the world until the present day a cruelty such as this hath neither been seen nor heard of.' 'He hath, during the greater part of His life, been sore-tried in the clutches of His enemies. His sufferings have now reached their culmination in this afflictive Prison, into which His oppressors have so unjustly thrown Him.'[15]

It would be in that prison, on 23 June 1870, after two years of imprisonment, when there were still no signs of any degree of freedom, that Mírzá Mihdí would offer his soul to God and with his father's blessing, would joyfully become a human ransom to bring happiness to the hearts of friends prevented from seeing their Beloved.

These and other themes related to the life of Mírzá Mihdí are elaborated in the chapters that follow.

3

Early Years in Tehran

Among the greatest women in the history of the Bahá'í Faith was Ásíyih Khánum, the saintly wife of Bahá'u'lláh and Mírzá Mihdí's mother. People who knew her during her life have given testimony to her exemplary character as the consort of Bahá'u'lláh, a faithful believer and devoted mother.

The Blessed Perfection called her Navváb [Highness] following a custom used by many Persian noblemen to refer to their wives. Navváb was also honoured with the designation the 'Most Exalted Leaf'. According to Shoghi Effendi, Navváb,

> . . . during almost forty years, continued to evince a fortitude, a piety, a devotion and a nobility of soul which earned her from the pen of her Lord the posthumous and unrivalled tribute of having been made His 'perpetual consort in all the worlds of God'.[1]

Navváb was the daughter of a wealthy vizier (minister) of the court of the Shah of Iran named Mírzá Ismá'íl of Yalrúd. Like her illustrious spouse, she belonged to the highest circles of the nobility. It was told that she was of great beauty and well educated, knowing how to write in Persian and Arabic. She was described, years later, as 'slender, stately . . . with white skin and blue eyes and dark hair'[2] and 'winsome, vivacious and exceedingly beautiful'.[3]

As stated earlier, her given name was Ásíyih, a name she shared with the most distinguished woman of the Faith of Moses, the wife[4] of the Egyptian Pharaoh, who, in the Islamic tradition, as a punishment for her belief in Moses, was laid with a heavy rock on her chest in the desert under the burning sun and tied down with four stakes.

The truly magnificent marriage of Navváb and Bahá'u'lláh occurred around October 1835. A specially hired jeweller worked at Ásíyih's house for six months on the bride's trousseau and dowry. To better understand the magnificence of the ceremony, suffice it to say that the buttons of the wedding dress were made of gold set with precious stones and that the trousseau was taken to the house of Bahá'u'lláh loaded on 40 mules. Such was the lavishness of the nuptials that for a long time the wedding was a topic of conversation in royal circles. Some time before, when Bahá'u'lláh's sister had married Navváb's brother, the festivities were so sumptuous that people remarked that they were 'adding wealth to wealth'.[5]

From this special marriage three spiritual jewels came into being, illuminating the world of humanity:

'Abdu'l-Bahá, Bahíyyih Khánum and Mírzá Mihdí. As mentioned above, there were four other children from this marriage who died very young, both before and after Bahá'u'lláh's exiles.

The material grandeur, however, never exceeded Navváb's spiritual greatness, which gave her a special glow. Her personal qualities were recognized by all: her beauty, her keen intelligence, her graceful charm and virtuosity. Her daughter, Bahíyyih Khánum, accompanied Navváb in all the tribulations that were heaped upon them in the lifetime of Bahá'u'lláh.

In a spoken chronicle, Bahíyyih Khánum related some features of her parents' brilliant personalities:

> I wish you could have seen her as I first remember her, tall, slender, graceful, eyes of dark blue – a pearl, a flower amongst women.
>
> I have been told that even when very young, her wisdom and intelligence were remarkable. I always think of her in those earliest days of my memory as queenly in her dignity and loveliness, full of consideration for everybody, gentle, of a marvellous unselfishness, no action of hers ever failed to show the loving-kindness of her pure heart; her very presence seemed to make an atmosphere of love and happiness wherever she came, enfolding all comers in the fragrance of gentle courtesy.
>
> Even in the early years of their married life, they,

my father and mother, took part as little as possible in State functions, social ceremonies, and the luxurious habits of ordinary highly-placed and wealthy families in the land of Persia; she, and her noble-hearted husband, counted these worldly pleasures meaningless, and preferred rather to occupy themselves in caring for the poor, and for all who were unhappy, or in trouble.

From our doors nobody was ever turned away; the hospitable board was spread for all comers.

Constantly the poor women came to my mother, to whom they poured out their various stories of woe, to be comforted and consoled by her loving helpfulness.

Whilst the people called my father 'The Father of the Poor', they spoke of my mother as 'The Mother of Consolation', though, naturally, only the women and little children ever looked upon her face unveiled.

So our peaceful days flowed on.

We used to go to our house in the country sometimes; my brother 'Abbás ['Abdu'l-Bahá] and I loved to play in the beautiful gardens, where grew many kinds of wonderful fruits and flowers and flowering trees; but this part of my early life is a very dim memory.[6]

Bahíyyih Khánum also described how such a comfortable environment was disrupted while living in Tehran, the capital of Persia. Her story describes the scenes of religious persecution that took place in the months following August 1852, two years after the martyrdom of the Báb.

One day I remember very well, though I was only six years old at the time. It seemed that an attempt had been made on the life of the S͟háh by a half-crazy young Bábí [follower of the Báb].

My father was away at his country house in the village of Níavirán, which was his property, the villagers of which were all and individually cared for by him.

Suddenly and hurriedly a servant came rushing in great distress to my mother.

'The master, the master, he is arrested – I have seen him! He has walked many miles! Oh, they have beaten him! They say he has suffered the torture of the bastinado! [Torture consisting of beating on the soles of the feet with a stick.] His feet are bleeding! He has no shoes on! His turban has gone! His clothes are torn! There are chains upon his neck!

My poor mother's face grew whiter and whiter.

We children were terribly frightened and could only weep bitterly.

Immediately everybody, all our relations, and friends, and servants fled from our house in terror, only one man-servant, Isfandiyár, remained, and one woman. Our palace, and the smaller houses belonging to it were very soon stripped of everything; furniture, treasures, all were stolen by the people.

MÍRZÁ MIHDÍ

Mírzá Músá, my father's brother, who was always very kind to us, helped my mother and her three children to escape into hiding. She succeeded in saving some few of the marriage treasures, which were all of our vast possessions left to us. These things were sold; with the money my mother was able to pay the gaolers to take food to my father in the prison, and to meet other expenses incurred later on.

We were now in a little house, not far from the prison. Mírzá Yáhyá (Ṣubḥ-i-Azal) had run away in terror to Mázindarán, where he remained in hiding.

Oh, the terrible anxiety my beloved mother suffered at that time! Surely greater than any woman, about to become a mother (as I afterwards knew), could possibly have strength to bear.

The prison [the Siyáh-Chál, the Black Pit] into which my father had been cast was a terrible place, seven steps below the ground; it was ankle-deep in filth, infested with horrible vermin, and of an indescribable loathsomeness. Added to this, there was no glimmer of light in that noisome place. Within its walls forty Bábís were crowded; murderers and highway robbers were also imprisoned there.

My noble father was hurled into this black hole, loaded with heavy chains; five other Bábís were chained to him night and day, and here he remained for four months. Picture to yourself the horror of these conditions.

Any movement caused the chains to cut deeper and deeper not only into the flesh of one, but of all who were chained together; whilst sleep or rest of any kind was not possible. No food was provided, and it was with the utmost difficulty that my mother was able to arrange to get any food or drink taken into that ghastly prison.

Meanwhile, the spirit which upheld the Bábís never quailed for a moment, even under these conditions. To be tortured to death, which would be the Martyr's Crown of Life, was their aim and great desire.

They chanted prayers night and day.

Every morning one or more of these brave and devoted friends would be taken out to be tortured and killed in various ways of horror.

When religious fanaticism was aroused against a person or persons, who were accused of being infidels, as was now the case with the Bábís, it was customary not simply to condemn them to death and have them executed by the State executioner, but to hand the victims over to various classes of the populace.

The butchers had their methods of torture; the bakers theirs; the shoemakers and blacksmiths yet others of their own. They were all given opportunities of carrying out their pitiless inventions on the Bábís.

The fanatics became more and more infuriated when they failed to quench the amazing spirit of these fearless, devoted ones, who remained unflinching, chanting prayers, asking God to pardon and bless their murderers, and praising Him, as long as they were able to breathe. The mob crowded to these fearful scenes, and yelled their execrations, whilst all through the fiendish work, a drum was loudly beaten.

These horrible sounds I well remember, as we three children clung to our mother, she not knowing whether the victim was her own adored husband. She could not find out whether he was still alive or not until late at night, or very early in the morning, when she determined to venture out, in defiance of the danger to herself and to us, for neither women or children were spared.

How well I remember cowering in the dark, with my little brother, Mírzá Mihdí, the Purest Branch, at that time two years old, in my arms, which were not very strong, as I was only six. I was shivering with terror, for I knew of some of the horrible things that were happening, and was aware that they might have seized even my mother.

So I waited and waited until she should come back. Then Mírzá Músá, my uncle, who was in hiding, would venture in to hear what tidings my mother had been able to gather.

My brother 'Abbás usually went with her on these sorrowful errands.

We listened eagerly to the accounts she gave to my uncle. This information came through the kindness of a sister of my grandfather, who was married to Mírzá Yúsif, a Russian subject, and a friend of the Russian Consul in Tehran. This gentleman, my great uncle by marriage, used to attend the courts to find out some particulars as to the victims chosen for execution day by day, and thus was able to relieve to some extent my mother's overwhelming anxiety as these appalling days passed over us.

It was Mírzá Yúsif who was able to help my mother about getting food taken to my father, and who brought us to the two little rooms near the prison, where we stayed in close hiding. He had to be very careful in thus defying the authorities, although the danger in this case was mitigated by the fact of his being under the protection of the Russian Consulate, as a Russian subject.

Nobody at all, of all our friends and relations, dared to come to see my mother during these days of death, but the wife of Mírzá Yúsif, the aunt of my father.

One day the discovery was made by Mírzá Yúsif that our untiring enemies, the most fanatical of the mullás [Muslim priests], were plotting the death of Mírzá Ḥusayn 'Alí Núrí [Bahá'u'lláh's name], my father.

Mírzá Yúsif consulted the Russian Consul; that powerful friend determined that this plan should be at once frustrated.

An amazing scene took place in the Court, where the sentences of death were passed. The Russian Consul rose and fearlessly addressed those in court:

'Hearken to me! I have words of importance to say to you' (his voice rang out, the president and officials were too amazed to reply).

'Have you not taken enough cruel revenge? Have you not already murdered a large enough number of harmless people, because of this accusation, of the absurd falseness of which you are quite aware? Has there not been sufficient of this orgy of brutal torture to satisfy you? How is it possible that you can even pretend to think that this august prisoner planned that silly attempt to shoot the Sháh?

'It is not unknown to you that the stupid gun, used by that poor youth, could not have killed a bird. Moreover, the boy was obviously insane. You know very well that this charge is not only untrue, but palpably ridiculous.

'There must be an end to all this.

'I have determined to extend the protection of Russia to this innocent nobleman; therefore beware! For if one hair of his head be hurt from this moment, *rivers of blood shall flow in your town as punishment.*

'You will do well to heed my warning, my country is behind me in this matter.'

An account of this scene was given to my mother by Mírzá Músá, when he came for tidings.

Needless to say how eagerly my brother and I listened, and how we all wept for joy.

Very soon afterwards we heard that, fearing to

disregard the stern warning of the Russian Consul, the Governor gave orders that my father should be permitted to come forth from that prison with his life. It was also decreed that he and his family were banished.

They were to leave Tehran for Baghdád. Ten days were allowed for preparation, as the beloved prisoner was very ill indeed.

And so he came to our two little rooms.

Oh, the joy of his presence!

Oh, the horror of that dungeon, where he had passed those four terrible months.

Jamál-i-Mubárak (a name given to my father, i.e. literally the Blessed Beauty) spoke very little of the terrible sufferings of that time! We, who saw the marks of what he had endured, where the chains had cut into the delicate skin, especially that of his neck, his wounded feet so long untended, evidence of the torture of the bastinado, how we wept with my dear mother.

He, on his part, told of the steadfast faith of the friends, who had gone forth to meet their death at the hands of their torturers, with joy and gladness, to attain the crown of martyrdom.

The glory had won so great a victory that the shame, and pain, and sorrow, and scorn were of comparatively no importance whatever!

Jamál-i-Mubárak had a marvellous divine experience whilst in that prison.

MÍRZÁ MIHDÍ

We saw a new radiance seeming to enfold him like a shining vesture, its significance we were to learn years later. At that time we were only aware of the wonder of it, without understanding, or even being told the details of the sacred event.

My mother did her best to nurse our beloved, that he might have some strength to set out upon that journey on which we were to start in ten days' time.

Now was a time of great difficulty.

How could she prepare?

The poor, dear lady sold almost all that remained of her marriage treasures, jewels, embroidered garments, and other belongings for which she received about four hundred túmáns. With this money she was able to make some provision for the terrible journey. (The Government provided nothing for those whom they exiled.)

This journey was filled with indescribable difficulties. My mother had no experience, no servants, no provisions, and very little money left. My father was extremely ill, not having recovered from the ordeals of the torture and the prison. No one of all of our friends and relations dared to come to our help, or even to say good-bye, but one old lady, the grandmother of Ásíyih Khánum.

Our faithful servant, Isfandiyár, and the one negro woman who did not fear to remain with us, did their best. But we three children were very young, my brother eight, and I six years old. Mírzá Mihdí, the 'Purest Branch', was very delicate, and my mother allowed herself to be persuaded to leave the little fellow, only two years old, with her grandmother, though the parting with him was very sad.

At length we started on that fearful journey, which lasted about four weeks;[7] the weather was bitterly cold, snow was upon the ground.

On the way to Baghdád we sometimes encamped in wilderness places, but in that month of December, the cold was intense, and we were not well prepared!

My poor mother! How she suffered on this journey, riding in a takht-i-raván, borne on a jolting mule! And this took place only six weeks before her youngest son was born!

Never did she utter one word of complaint. She was always thinking of some kindness for somebody, and sympathy she gave unsparingly to all in their difficulties.[8]

4

Exile in Baghdad, Constantinople and Adrianople

Long before the persecutions, while in Tehran, Navváb had opened her house to the Faith. In those years Bahá'u'lláh had become the champion of the Faith of the Báb, constantly visiting, often on horseback, the various towns and villages of His native province and other regions, spreading the new teachings, encouraging the believers in historical events such as the siege of Ṭabarsí and the Conference of Badasht.

Their splendid residence in Tehran was the pivot of the activities of the friends. Distinguished believers such as Mullá Ḥusayn, Quddús, Vaḥíd, Hujjat and Ṭáhirih visited them. Nabíl, the leading historian of the Faith, remembered once being cured of an eye condition with an ointment prepared by her. Navváb also associated with Ṭáhirih, a brilliant believer and poet who for some time lived at their home.

Bahá'u'lláh was often away from home promoting the interests of the Cause of the Báb. His material and spiritual help was always needed by the nascent community of believers struggling to grow in an environment of bigotry and intolerance. Three times He was imprisoned on Persian soil and he was tortured until He bled. He bore the weight of 50-kilogram chains, was deprived of food and drink and was stripped of His earthly possessions. And when, by the decree of the Shah of Iran, the Holy Family had to cross the country's borders forever, Navváb never looked back and willingly exchanged the amenities that wealth had enabled her to enjoy for a sequence of interminable difficulties and a life of uncertainty and hardship brought by successive exiles in foreign lands. These exiles were to Baghdad in 1853, Constantinople and Adrianople in 1863 and finally the Most Great Prison in 'Akká in 1868.

In her spoken chronicle Bahíyyih Khánum recounted the incidents of this exile to Baghdad where her mother, who had lived a life of comfort and luxury, had to manage without servants:

> When we came to a city, my dear mother would take the clothes and wash them at the public baths; we also were able to have baths at those places. She would carry the cold, wet clothes away in her arms – drying them was an almost impossible task; her lovely hands, being unused to such coarse work, became very painful.
>
> We sometimes stayed at a caravanserai – a sort of rough inn. Only one room was allowed for one family,

and for one night – no longer. No light was permitted at night, and there were no beds. Sometimes we were able to have tea, or again a few eggs, a little cheese, and some coarse bread.

My father was so ill that he could not eat the rough food – my mother was very distressed and tried to think of some way of getting different food, as he grew more weak through eating nothing.

One day she had been able to get a little flour, and at night, when we arrived at the caravanserai she made a sweet cake for him. Alas! – the misfortune – being dark, she used salt instead of sugar. So the cake was uneatable! Quite a tragedy in its way.

The Governor of Tihrán sent soldiers with us to the frontier, where Turkish soldiers met us and escorted us to Baghdád.

When we first arrived there, we had a very little house, consisting of my father's room, and another one which was my mother's and in which were also my eldest brother, the baby, and myself.

When Arab ladies came to see us, this was the only reception room. These ladies came because they had been taught by Táhirih, Qurratu'l-'Ayn, during her visit to Baghdád.

One day when an old lady was there, I was told to prepare the samovár [a metal urn used to heat water and prepare tea] – it was very heavy to carry upstairs, for my arms were not extremely strong. The old lady said: 'One proof that the Bábí teaching is wonderful is that a very little girl served the samovár!'

My father was amused, he used to say, 'Here is the lady converted by seeing your service at the samovár!'

Among the Arabians taught by Táhirih was Shaykh Sultán, whose daughter married Mírzá Músá, brother of Bahá'u'lláh. Their daughter eventually married Muḥammad-'Alí, half-brother of 'Abdu'l-Bahá.

Mírzá Músá and his wife were always devoted to Bahá'u'lláh. This uncle, Mírzá Músá, who came into exile with us, was a very kind helper in everything. At one time he did almost all the cooking, for which he had a talent; he would also help with the washing.

Ásíyih Khánum, my dear mother, was in delicate health, her strength was diminished by the hardships she had undergone, but she always worked beyond her force.

Sometimes my father himself helped in the cooking, as that hard work was too much for the dainty, refined, gentle lady. The hardships she had endured saddened the heart of her divine husband, who was also her beloved Lord.[1]

The Holy Family moved into 'an extremely modest residence situated in the Karkh quarter, in the neighbourhood of the western bank of the river'.[2] The reception room used by Bahá'u'lláh was very simple, with a low roof and constructed of mud and straw and adorned with a small garden. It was furnished with a single sofa made out of palm branches where Bahá'u'lláh used to sit. Such was the poverty that His clothes had to be washed and dried at night for use the next day, as this was all that He had. This house was later declared by the Blessed Beauty to be a place of pilgrimage. Many believers of Persia as well as princes, peasants, theologians, the rich and the poor began to visit the house and look for the presence of Bahá'u'lláh. Mírzá Mihdí, growing as an adolescent, must have learned a lot about his father and His Cause in that historical residence, which Bahá'u'lláh referred to as the Most Great House and the House of God. About the glory of this sacred house He wrote to a believer:

> When thou art departed out of the court of My presence, O Muḥammad, direct thy steps towards My House (Baghdád House), and visit it on behalf of thy Lord. When thou reachest its door, stand thou before it and say: Whither is the Ancient Beauty gone, O most great House of God, He through Whom God hath made thee the cynosure of an adoring world, and proclaimed thee to be the sign of His remembrance unto all who are in the heavens and all who are on the earth? Oh! for the former days when thou, O House of God, wert made His footstool, the days when in ceaseless strains the melody of the All-Merciful poured

Násiri'd-Dín Sháh of Iran (1848–96)

Sulṭán 'Abdu'l-Azíz of the Ottoman Empire (1830–76)

A view of Tehran in the time of Mírzá Mihdí

Historical view of Baghdad and the Tigris River

The bridge at Büyükçekmece, Turkey, over which Mírzá Mihdí crossed with his father Bahá'u'lláh, his family and their companions on their way from Constantinople to Adrianople in December 1863

One of the houses in which Mírzá Mihdí lived with Bahá'u'lláh and His family in Adrianople

A group of exiled Bahá'ís in Adrianople. Mírzá Mihdí and 'Abdu'l-Bahá are seated second and third from the left

Detail from the picture above, showing Mírzá Mihdí, left, with his brother 'Abdu'l-Bahá, in Adrianople

Bahíyyih <u>Kh</u>ánum, The Greatest Holy Leaf, in Adrianople

The Arciduca Ferdinando Massimiliano, *built in 1856, in which Mírzá Mihdí, Bahá'u'lláh and His family and companions may have travelled from Gallipoli to Haifa*

Passengers on the Deck of a Steam Packet in the Adriatic Sea
by Henry Burdon Richardson

The sea gate through which Mírzá Mihdí entered 'Akká with Bahá'u'lláh, the family and companions in 1868

A street in 'Akká, typical of those along which Mírzá Mihdí walked with Bahá'u'lláh and the exiles to the barracks

When they first arrived at the citadel, Bahá'u'lláh, Mírzá Mihdí and the other exiles were taken to rooms adjoining the barracks square

Layout of the prison

'Akká

The citadel in 'Akká

forth from thee! What hath become of thy jewel whose glory hath irradiated all creation? Whither are gone the days in which He, the Ancient King, had made thee the throne of His glory, the days in which He had chosen thee alone to be the lamp of salvation between earth and heaven, and caused thee to diffuse, at dawn and at eventide, the sweet fragrance of the All-Glorious?

Where, O House of God, is the Sun of majesty and power Who had enveloped thee with the brightness of His presence? Where is He, the Day Spring of the tender mercies of thy Lord, the Unconstrained, Who had established His seat within thy walls? What is it, O throne of God, that hath altered thy countenance, and made thy pillars to tremble? What could have closed thy door to the face of them that eagerly seek thee? What hath made thee so desolate? Couldst thou have been told that the Beloved of the world is pursued by the swords of His enemies? The Lord bless thee, and bless thy fidelity unto Him, inasmuch as thou hast remained His companion through all His sorrows and His sufferings.

I testify that thou art the scene of His transcendent glory, His most holy habitation. Out of thee hath gone forth the Breath of the All-Glorious, a Breath that hath breathed over all created things, and filled with joy the breasts of the devout that dwell in the mansions of Paradise. The Concourse on high, and they that inhabit the Cities of the Names of God, weep over thee, and bewail the things that have befallen thee.

Thou art still the symbol of the names and attributes of the Almighty, the Point towards which the eyes of the Lord of earth and heaven are directed. There hath befallen thee what hath befallen the Ark in which God's pledge of security had been made to dwell. Well is it with him that apprehendeth the intent of these words, and recognizeth the purpose of Him Who is the Lord of all creation.

Happy are those that inhale from thee the sweet savours of the Merciful, that acknowledge thine exaltation, that safeguard thy sanctity, that reverence, at all times, thy station. We implore the Almighty to grant that the eyes of those who have turned away from thee, and failed to appreciate thy worth, may be opened, that they may truly recognize thee, and Him Who, through the power of truth, hath raised thee up on high. Blind, indeed, are they about thee, and utterly unaware of thee in this day. Thy Lord is, verily, the Gracious, the Forgiving.

I bear witness that through thee God hath proved the hearts of His servants. Blessed be the man that directeth his steps toward thee, and visiteth thee. Woe to him that denieth thy right, that turneth away from thee, that dishonoureth thy name, and profaneth thy holiness.[3]

Despite their poverty, there was always a plate of food to be shared by the Holy Family with their numerous visitors. 'Abdu'l-Bahá many years later said:

> Contentment is real wealth. If one develops within himself the quality of contentment he will become independent. Contentment is the creator of happiness. When one is contented he does not care either for riches or poverty. He lives above the influence of them and is indifferent to them. When we were in Baghdad often with one pound of meat we served dinner to fifteen or twenty people. We cooked with it Persian stew and filled the pot with water so everyone could have a bowl of soup. Notwithstanding this we were all very happy and thought that ours was the most delicious dinner.[4]

The happiness of those days was crowned when Mírzá Mihdí was brought from Iran at about 11 years of age. The Holy Family remained in Baghdad for a period of ten years. During all that time the spiritual ascendancy of the Blessed Beauty grew in fame and the reputation of His wisdom and holiness spread throughout the city. This, however, aroused the jealousy of the opponents of the Cause who were constantly monitoring the activities of the exiles. Through their influence these ill-wishers persuaded the Turkish government to call Bahá'u'lláh to the city of Constantinople, capital of the empire.

The order of the Sultan 'Abdu'l-Azíz of Turkey, with

the support of the Shah of Iran, broke the relative peace that the Holy Family had begun to enjoy. Before leaving Baghdad for Constantinople, Bahá'u'lláh retired for 12 days to the Garden of Riḍván on the outskirts of the city where He declared His prophetic mission to a number of believers and the family.

Details about this momentous event in which Mírzá Mihdí participated were left by 'Abdu'l-Bahá:

> During the nights of those days we could not sleep because we fancied in our minds the unparalleled joy of meeting Baha'o'llah in the morning, standing in his presence, receiving his graces, and listening to his words. It was on the ninth day that the Blessed Perfection leaving Baghdad stayed in the Garden of Hajib Pasha before starting for Constantinople. It is impossible to describe with words the beatific vibrations with which we were surrounded in those days. Although to all outward appearances the Blessed Perfection was in exile, yet he moved with such power and manifested such majesty! The list of visitors calling on him during these ten days looks rather like the roll call of an army. Those who had never seen him while he lived in Baghdad called. All the leaders of the community, the officers of the army, and of the government paid a visit. Even the Governor, Najib Pasha, called and Baha'o'llah did not return these rather important calls. Were one to reflect for a moment

he would realize that such great events have never occurred in the history of the past dispensations![5]

The journey to Constantinople, now Istanbul, took more than three months by land and sea, throughout which they were accompanied by officers and guards. Bahá'u'lláh and his family disembarked from the steamer on Sunday, 16 August 1863.

Istanbul was in the eyes of any ordinary traveller a fascinating city from a material point of view. The third largest city in the world, after London and Paris, it was inhabited by a cosmopolitan population spread on two continents, Asia and Europe, on each side of the Bosphorus Strait. The city had been undergoing a process of modernization which included splendid buildings, running water and electricity, large bridges, the telegraph, big ports, horse dawn trams and steam ferry services among other facilities developed in the 19th century. It was also the cultural centre for the region, attracting brilliant minds in the sciences, humanities and music including trade fairs and industrial exhibitions. Its architecture was amazing, with beautiful, large and beautiful mosques such as the Blue and the Suleymaniye mosques, the Great Bazaar – the largest covered market in the world – churches such as the cathedral of Sacred Sofia (Hagia Sophia) as well as other edifices built by native and European architects. Istanbul was called the 'Dome of Islam', the 'Sublime

Porte', the 'Great City', the seat of the Sultan, where all the great world powers where represented.

Situated between two seas, the Marmara and the Black Sea, the city sustained an intense centre of commercial exchange between the East and the West. The visitor who tours the 45,000 square metre Dolmabahçe Palace opened in 1856 with its 285 rooms and 46 halls can see how the reigning Sultan 'Abdu'l-Azíz and his court lived in great splendour and lavishness. However, in contrast to these material magnificences, Bahá'u'lláh described the spiritual environment involving this city in stern terms:

> Narrate, O Servant, the things Thou didst behold at the time of Thine arrival in the City, that Thy testimony may endure amongst men, and serve as a warning unto them that believe. We found, upon Our arrival in the City, its governors and elders as children gathered about and disporting themselves with clay. We perceived no one sufficiently mature to acquire from Us the truths which God hath taught Us, nor ripe for Our wondrous words of wisdom. Our inner eye wept sore over them, and over their transgressions and their total disregard of the thing for which they were created. This is what We observed in that City, and which We have chosen to note down in Our Book, that it may serve as a warning unto them, and unto the rest of mankind.[6]

After a four month sojourn in Istanbul, the Blessed Beauty and His family received a second, unannounced, decree of exile from Sultan 'Abdu'l-Azíz. This time they went to Adrianople, presently known as Edirne, approximately 250 km away. During the trip in the middle of winter the companions suffered such intense cold that they had to light bonfires to melt the ice from the springs in order to obtain water. The march through heavy rain and storms to the new place of exile continued even at night.

Bahá'u'lláh referred to Adrianople as 'the place which none entereth except such as have rebelled against the authority of the sovereign'. 'They expelled Us from the city (Constantinople)', He addressed the Sultan, 'with an abasement with which no abasement on earth can compare.' 'Neither My family, nor those who accompanied Me, had the necessary raiment to protect them from the cold in that freezing weather.' 'The eyes of Our enemies wept over Us, and beyond them those of every discerning person.'[7] Upon their arrival they were settled at an inn for travellers, but were moved shortly afterwards to one house, then another and finally, after about ten months, a third. Poverty prevailed and at times the only food in the house was bread and cheese.

While the Sultan and his court lived in the utmost opulence, the Holy Family was barely surviving under extreme conditions. Yet incomparably exalted above the glamour of the Dolmabahçe Palace, built at a cost equivalent to 35 tonnes of gold, with its 600 metre long facade facing the calm and blue Bosphorus, was the small rented house located on a narrow street of Adrianople; it was supremely ennobled by the presence of Bahá'u'lláh, the King of Kings, who was later described by Professor Edward Granville Browne of Cambridge University in these poignant words:

> Those piercing eyes seemed to read one's very soul; power and authority sat on that ample brow; while the deep lines on the forehead and face implied an age which the jet-black hair and beard flowing down in indistinguishable luxuriance almost to the waist seemed to belie. No need to ask in whose presence I stood, as I bowed myself before one who is the object of a devotion and love which kings might envy and emperors sigh for in vain![8]

Likewise, Mírzá Ḥaydar-'Alí, a Bahá'í who attained the presence of Bahá'u'lláh, related:

> . . . when I beheld the light of His beauteous Countenance, I was transported into such a state that all the miracles I had hoped to see and all the physical and spiritual mysteries I had longed to understand, paled into insignificance. They all appeared to me as a mirage to which the thirsty hasten, not the pure water

which quenches the thirst and gives life . . . His blessed person appeared in the form of a human being, but His very movements, His manners, His way of sitting or standing, eating or drinking, even His sleep or wakefulness, were each a miracle to me. Because His perfections, His exalted character, His beauty, His glory, His most excellent titles and most august attributes revealed to me that He was peerless and without parallel. He was matchless with no one to join partners with Him, unique with no peer or equal, the One and Single without a deputy, the Ever-Abiding God, the Incomparable Being. He who 'begetteth not, neither is He begotten and there is not anyone like unto Him'.

. . . I saw a Person Who, from the human point of view, was like the rest of humanity. However, if one were to add the love, mercy and compassion of all the peoples of the world together, it would appear as a drop when compared with the ocean of His tender mercy and loving-kindness. I even seek God's forgiveness for making such a comparison. Similarly, if one brought together all the knowledge of sciences, crafts, philosophy, politics, natural history and divinity possessed by mankind, it would seem, in comparison with His knowledge and understanding, as an atom compared to the sun. If one weighed the might and power of kings, rulers, Prophets and Messengers against His omnipotence and sovereignty, His grandeur and glory,

His majesty and dominion, they would be as insignificant as a touch of moisture compared with the waters of the sea ... As I observed every one of His attributes, I discovered my inability to emulate Him, and realized that all the peoples of the world will never be able to attain to His perfections.[9]

It was from Adrianople (now Edirne), located in Western Europe, inhabited mostly by Christians, that Bahá'u'lláh addressed His historic and momentous summons to the kings and rulers of the earth. Also, many pilgrims from Iran were able to reach Adrianople and attain the presence of the Blessed Beauty.

The Holy Family and the group of exiles remained in Adrianople for about five years before being sent to the prison of 'Akká which was part of Ottoman Syria at the time.

The exiles' permanency in Adrianople was seriously disturbed when, after a time, Covenant-breakers – enemies of the Faith – headed by Mírzá Yaḥyá, unleashed a campaign of public calumnies against Bahá'u'lláh. His half-brother, claiming to be the Báb's successor and leader of the community of believers and poisoned with his own jealousy of Bahá'u'lláh's fame, plotted to kill Him on several occasions, one of which has been described by Shoghi Effendi, the Guardian of the Faith:

Desperate designs to poison Bahá'u'lláh and His companions, and thereby reanimate his own defunct leadership, began, approximately a year after their arrival in Adrianople, to agitate his mind. Well aware of the erudition of his half-brother, Áqáy-i-Kalím, in matters pertaining to medicine, he, under various pretexts, sought enlightenment from him regarding the effects of certain herbs and poisons, and then began, contrary to his wont, to invite Bahá'u'lláh to his home, where, one day, having smeared His tea-cup with a substance he had concocted, he succeeded in poisoning Him sufficiently to produce a serious illness which lasted no less than a month, and which was accompanied by severe pains and high fever, the aftermath of which left Bahá'u'lláh with a shaking hand till the end of His life. So grave was His condition that a foreign doctor, named Shíshmán, was called in to attend Him. The doctor was so appalled by His livid hue that he deemed His case hopeless, and, after having fallen at His feet, retired from His presence without prescribing a remedy. A few days later that doctor fell ill and died. Prior to his death Bahá'u'lláh had intimated that doctor Shíshmán had sacrificed his life for Him. To Mírzá Áqá Ján, sent by Bahá'u'lláh to visit him, the doctor had stated that God had answered his prayers, and that after his death a certain Dr. Chupán, whom he knew to be reliable, should, whenever necessary, be called in his stead.[10]

On another occasion Mírzá Yaḥyá poisoned the well from which the Holy Family drew water for their daily consumption. Using all means at his disposal to gain leadership of the community, Mírzá Yaḥyá tried to discredit Bahá'u'lláh among the government and the citizens. To his despair, he realized that most believers turned towards Bahá'u'lláh rather than to him. Mírzá Mihdí's spiritual acumen was revealed at a young age when he noted, 'This journey has taught us many things. For example, Azal [Mírzá Yaḥyá] believed that everyone would be subservient to him, and yet he now sees that such is not the case.'[11]

At the same time, other opponents of the Faith took advantage of the campaign to unleash their own bigotry. In the end, this series of events precipitated a serious crisis and the Sultan quickly seized the opportunity to issue the decree for Bahá'u'lláh's third banishment.

On 26 July 1868 the Sultan of Turkey signed an edict banishing Bahá'u'lláh and five others[12] from Adrianople. Bahá'u'lláh's family and a group of Bahá'ís, including extended families with children, were prepared to go with Him and share His imprisonment. However, the final place of banishment was not disclosed to them at that time but only later, when, after many days, they were at sea on their way to 'Akká. In various Tablets revealed in Adrianople, Bahá'u'lláh had alluded to 'Akká as the place of His future exile.[13]

The pain of the Holy Family reached its maximum

point. The court ministers, the monarch himself and the Persian ambassador issued instructions that the confinement should be strictly enforced. But this edict was not unexpected. As attested by Shoghi Effendi, Bahá'u'lláh Himself, as far back as the first year of His residence in Adrianople, had alluded in symbolic language to His eventual banishment to 'Akká, predicting that 'Upon our arrival, We were welcomed with banners of light, whereupon the Voice of the Spirit cried out saying: "Soon will all that dwell on earth be enlisted under these banners."'[14]

5

The Long Journey to 'Akká

The land and sea journey from Adrianople to 'Akká took 19 days. It was an odyssey characterized by the uncertainty of the final destination, plying through the Mediterranean Sea in three different vessels, in crowded compartments, living on prisoners' rations and travelling under the heat of the season. It was marked by the passing of one of the believers but also, on a more positive note, the surprise of finding Nabíl, the future great historian of the Bahá'í Faith, whose exact detention location in Egypt was unknown until then.

Details of the miserable trip from Adrianople to 'Akká have been left to posterity by Bahíyyih Khánum, Mírzá Mihdí's sister:

> During the period of his residence at Adrianople, Abbas Effendi had endeared himself to every one, high and low, those of the faith and others alike. He taught much and even at that time was commonly called the 'Master'. The Governor himself had become a friend of the Master's and delighted to listen to his

religious discourses. It was the habit of the Governor frequently to have the Master at the palace, and when my brother could not go to the Governor he sometimes came to my brother.

When the Governor received the order of banishment from Adrianople he was so affected by it that, not having the heart to execute it himself, he put it into the hands of his subordinates for execution, wrote a letter to Abbas Effendi, and left the city. In this letter he said:

'This trouble has come upon you through members of your own family. It is Subh i Ezel who has caused the Sultan to take these steps. I am powerless to aid you, and my love for you is so great that I must go away. I cannot see this dreadful thing happen.'

This trouble broke with the suddenness of a tornado upon us. We were sitting quietly together at home when we heard a bugle-call. My brother ['Abdu'l-Bahá] looked out and saw a cordon of soldiers about the house presenting arms. Our first thought was that the life of the Blessed Perfection or of Abbas Effendi was threatened. The latter endeavoured to quiet our alarm, and went out to inquire the cause of this demonstration. He was given the Governor's letter. The family consulted and Abbas Effendi then told the officer in command that we would die rather than be separated, and asked at least for respite. The reply was, 'No; you must go to-day, Beha Ullah and his family to different places, and neither can know the destination of the other.' Abbas Effendi demanded permission to go to the Governor's palace and appeal to his representative. This was at first refused but finally granted, and he set out between two guards.

My brother pleaded so eloquently with the officials that they consented to telegraph to Constantinople asking that the order be changed so that our family might remain together. A reply was received refusing the change. My brother persisted, and had such influence with the officials that they seemed unable to put the measure into execution, permitting him to send despatch after despatch for a week.

These were days of horror. The members of our family neither ate nor slept. No cooking was done in the house. When my brother left in the morning with the guards we feared that we might never see him again, and watched hour after hour for his return.

At length a telegram was received granting the concession that my father should be permitted to take with him his immediate family, but directing that his followers should be separated from him, without knowledge of his destination. A servant who had accompanied my brother overheard a part of this despatch read and misunderstood it. Without waiting to inquire whether he had heard aright, he returned to us with the report that the first order was not to be rescinded; that the Blessed Perfection was to be separated from his family and his followers. After telling us this he ran out and spread the news among the believers who were gathered near our house. They were as though stunned, paralysed. One of them, an old and faithful follower, seized a knife, and exclaiming, 'If I must be separated from my Lord, I will go now and join my God,' cut his throat. Fortunately this man's knife was partially arrested by a bystander so that his jugular vein was not severed; with the aid of a physician his life was ultimately saved.

The attempted suicide caused a great noise and disturbance, which attracted our attention. My mother and I went out to inquire into the cause of the commotion. We came near, and saw a man lying on the ground with blood streaming from him. The soldiers surrounding the group prevented us from approaching closely enough to determine with certainty who it was, but the first thought which came to us was that my poor brother, on hearing that the order was to be carried out, had, in his despair, killed himself. We could hear the gulping utterances of the man – 'You have separated me from my Lord, – I prefer to die.' Though unable to distinguish the voice, we still thought it was my brother. We remained in this agonising suspense for some time, until we suddenly heard my brother's voice rising high above the din, and speaking with tremendous force.

On hearing him, two things amazed us. First, he seemed to be wrought up to the highest pitch of anger and indignation. Never before had we heard him speak an angry word. We had known him sometimes impatient and peremptory, but never angry. And then, his great excitement had apparently given him command of the Turkish language, which no one had ever heard him speak before. He was, in Turkish, and in the most impassioned and vehement manner, protesting against, and denouncing, the treatment of the officers and demanding the presence of the Governor, who in the meantime had returned to the city. The officers seemed cowed by his vehemence, and the Governor was sent for. He came, and seeing the situation said, 'It is impossible, we cannot separate these people.'

The Governor returned to his palace and telegraphed to Constantinople. The next day he received a reply granting permission to the followers of the Blessed Perfection to accompany him. We were told to prepare for immediate departure, but were not told to what place we were to be sent. When we set out there were seventy-seven in all in our band. We journeyed six days, and arrived at Gallipoli, which is on the sea.

On our arrival at this town we were met with the information that the Governor had a telegraphic order from the Sultan's government directing our separation; that my father with one servant was to go to one place, my brother with one servant to another, the family to Constantinople, the other followers to various places. This sudden and unexplained withdrawal of the hard-won concession we had so recently obtained exhausted our patience. We unhesitatingly declared that we would not be separated, and a repetition, in substance, of the events of the last days in Adrianople followed. My brother went to the Governor and told him that we would not submit to separation. 'Do this,' said he, – 'take us out on a steamer and drown us in the ocean. You can thus end at once our sufferings and your perplexities. But we refuse to be separated.'

We remained in Gallipoli for a week, in the same horrible suspense which we had experienced at Adrianople. Finally my brother, by his eloquence in argument and power of will, succeeded in gaining for the second time from the Constantinople government the concession that we should remain together.

At Gallipoli the German, Russian, and English Consuls called upon the Blessed Perfection and offered to intercede in his behalf with the Turkish government, assuring him that they could procure, for him and his family, permission to go to one of the countries of Western Europe, where they would have no further trouble. My father replied that he did not wish to oppose the will of the Sultan, nor would he consent to abandon his followers; that his only interests were in spiritual things and his only desire to preach a religion, and that therefore he had nothing to fear.

The order from Constantinople directed that we should embark together upon a government vessel, and no time was lost in putting it into execution.[1]

Steamers were the vessels of that time. Steamers provided commercial transportation of passengers, cargo, mail and even horses across port cities on the Mediterranean Sea. To appreciate the difficulties of the exiles' journey, consider what sea travel was like before 1868 around the Mediterranean Sea and the passage to British colonies overseas. For example, en route to India, Australia and Hong Kong, passengers had to disembark at Alexandria, on the Mediterranean side of Egypt, traverse about 300 km of that country by train in order to board another steamer at the Red Sea and from there gain access to the Indian Ocean and Pacific Ocean. However, from 1869, the Suez Canal connected the Mediterranean and the Red Sea, greatly shortening the journey and creating strategic routes between Europe and Asia, the West and the East.

The steamships would navigate day and night accompanied by the monotonous sound of the paddlewheel crashing through the water and occasional whistles, sirens and bells. While the privileged were hosted in elegant staterooms with all facilities and top quality food and drinks, passengers in the lower classes were accommodated in cramped compartments with bunk beds that also served as lounge rooms, ate on long tables and shared filthy amenities sometimes plagued with insects and even rats.

While representing a shortening of travel time over land transportation, the amenities provided by steamships were not ideal when compared to modern standards. For example, over-crowded cabins that had to be shared with other people were priced differently for first, second and third class passengers. The coal-powered engines generated excessive smoke, frequently requiring passengers to remain inside their smart compartments to avoid the smell and carbon dust. These new technologies, products of the industrial revolution, were, however, fostering a new tourism industry, and international travel from the West towards the East increased understanding of nations and cultures. With agencies in many parts of the world, these steamship companies, like modern airlines, competed with one another by advertising their fares and tours to exotic countries.

Shoghi Effendi, the Guardian of the Bahá'í Faith, commented on the tense moments before the embarkation of the exiles on the Austrian Lloyd steamship:

> So grievous were the dangers and trials confronting Bahá'u'lláh at the hour of His departure from Gallipoli that He warned His companions that 'this journey will be unlike any of the previous journeys', and that whoever did not feel himself 'man enough to face the future' had best 'depart to whatever place he pleaseth, and be preserved from tests, for hereafter he will find himself unable to leave' – a warning which His companions unanimously chose to disregard.[2]

The Hand of the Cause of God Abu'l-Qasim Faizi wrote about those stressful moments and how this large group of people undertook the trip in a small vessel from Gallipoli to Alexandria, the first leg of the journey to Palestine, escorted by ten officers and soldiers:

> To reach the Austrian boat which had anchored far away from the shore the passengers had to cross in small sailing boats. At the same time that Bahá'u'lláh was entering one of those boats He was already uttering verses. Jináb-i-Anís and his companions were standing on the shore watching their Beloved on His way to a destination as yet undisclosed; a poignant sorrow pressed their hearts and tears flowed down their cheeks. Bahá'u'lláh, beholding them thus stricken with grief, consoled them and strengthened their hearts by showering His love and compassion upon them. Thus He cheered the burning hearts of His lovers throughout the world in their moments of grief and separation.[3]

The group departed Gallipoli for Alexandria in Egypt before noon on 21 August 1868. 'Abdu'l-Bahá is reported to have written that 'they put us on board a ship and made us pay most of the passage money'.[4] Áqá Riḍá wrote about starting the journey from Gallipoli, 'On an evening our luggage was taken to the ship, and the next morning boats took us aboard . . .'[5] And Bahíyyih Khánum, Mírzá Mihdí's sister, related many years later, 'We had embarked so hurriedly that we had been unable to provide for the voyage – a few loaves and a little cheese, brought by one of the friends, was all the food we had for those indescribable days.'[6]

Research undertaken by Kent Beveridge suggests that the steamers from Gallipoli to Alexandria and from Alexandria to Haifa in Palestine might have been the *Arciduca Ferdinando Massimiliano* and the *Saturno*. The *Arciduca Ferdinando Massimiliano*, built in 1856, could accommodate 48 first class and 28 second class passengers with a crew of 25 staff. In turn, the *Saturno*, which had begun service only four months before the Bahá'ís travelled to Haifa, was a larger vessel accommodating 51 first class, 28 second class passengers and a crew of 40. The former was described as a ship with paddlewheels while the latter was a more modern propeller vessel with auxiliary sails. Both were iron ships built in the United Kingdom and belonged to the Austrian Lloyd fleet which consisted of 64 steamships by 1867.[7] Whichever one was taken, both the ships must have been over-capacity, as the exiles themselves were over 80 in number, let alone the other travellers. Sixty-seven of them,[8] mostly Bahá'u'lláh's followers, were destined for 'Akká, while 16 people,[9] mostly followers of Mírzá Yaḥyá, were sent to Cyprus, 300 km further away.

To escape the tedium of the journey, passengers had to emerge through the companionway towards the upper desk – the only place to stretch their legs, have a look at the immensity of the so-called Great Sea, enjoy sporadic views of the coast or perhaps interact with travellers from other latitudes. The interminable parade of hours of daylight were followed only by the dullness of the night, the travel at all times marked by the swaying of the wooden craft and the roughness of the waters.

Ironically, inside the ship its passengers were uninterested in the Divine Personage. No one seemed to care particularly when they were labelled as government prisoners being transported to their place of imprisonment and under the constant watch of military officers. The few Persians aboard were too busy looking after their own consul who was moving to his post in the port city of Smyrna with all honours. According to Abu'l-Qasim Faizi, 'Boarding the Austrian steamer they found passengers, including some Persians. Bahá'u'lláh did not talk to anyone, but went ahead to a spacious place where several chairs were arranged. He occupied one of these chairs and permitted the friends to take their seats too.'[10] It is noteworthy that the uncertainty of the destination was exacerbated by the hostile presence in the ship of the sinister Mírzá Yaḥyá, his family and some of his followers. Mírzá Yaḥyá would stay with the group until

Haifa, after which he was going to be confined on the island of Cyprus.

Providence manifested itself through the multitude of stars gazing lovingly upon our exiles, abandoned by the world in the middle of nowhere, men and women, the elderly and children, en route to a remote, undisclosed and mysterious location, clinging fervently to the protection of their Lord, the true Master of the ship. He Himself had reassured everyone at the beginning of the trip in Gallipoli that the ship would 'not sink, even if it is battered by all the waves'.[11]

The vessel arrived in Mytilene (called Madellí by the Persians) on the Greek island of Lebos by sunset and later in the evening left for Smyrna, where the exiles stayed two days. One of the believers, Jináb-i-Muníb, became very sick. According to 'Abdu'l-Bahá:

> He had been stricken by a severe ailment and was pitifully weak. Still, he would not agree to remaining behind in Adrianople where he could receive treatment, because he wanted to sacrifice his life and fall at the feet of his Lord. We journeyed along till we reached the sea. He was now so feeble that it took three men to lift him and carry him onto the ship. Once he was on board, his condition grew so much worse that the captain insisted we put him off the ship, but because of our repeated pleas he waited till we reached Smyrna. In Smyrna, the captain addressed Colonel 'Umar

Bayk, the government agent who accompanied us, and told him: 'If you don't put him ashore, I will do it by force, because the ship will not accept passengers in this condition.'[12]

He was taken to the local hospital on Smyrna. The believers were allowed to be with him for only one hour. According to Bahíyyih Khánum:

> The Master bought a melon and some grapes; returning with the refreshing fruit for him – He found that he had died. Arrangements were made with the director of the hospital for a simple funeral. The Master chanted some prayers, then, heartsore, came back to the boat.[13]

With one less companion, the group then continued the journey to Alexandria, on the other shore of the Mediterranean Sea, moving from the European to the African continent. They arrived in Alexandria, an important regional port situated on the Nile delta, two days later, in the morning. In Alexandria the group was transhipped to another Austrian Lloyd steamer and rumours were spread that they would be dispersed to different destinations. We do not know for certain whether Bahá'u'lláh was transhipped boat-to-boat or via the shore. However, as recounted in the next pages, the nearness of the ship from the shore suggests that

He was able to put His blessed feet on Egyptian soil, if only for a very short time.

Bahíyyih Khánum's narrative continues:

> In the hurry, distress, and uncertainty of the moment, we neglected to provide food for the voyage [at Gallipoli], but to one old servant, on his way to the ship, the thought occurred that he had not seen any provisions prepared, and he bought a box of bread. This, with the ship's prisoners' rations, which were almost inedible, was the only food we had for five days, when we reached Alexandria. Here the rumour that we were to be separated was renewed; and all were so terrified by it that no one was willing to leave the ship to buy provisions lest he be prevented from returning. We were able to procure only some grapes and mineral water.
>
> The little bread we had was now spoiled; and, what with hunger, fright, and grief, we were almost bereft of reason.[14]

Interestingly, in Alexandria, Nabíl, the great Bahá'í historian, was imprisoned because of his beliefs. In prison he had had a dream in which the Blessed Beauty had come to him and told him that 'Within the next eighty-one days, to thee will come some cause of rejoicing'.[15] The anticipated day came. While Nabíl was on the prison roof around sunset, he suddenly noticed one of the exiles walking on the street below, escorted by a policeman. An acquaintance of Nabíl, this believer was going back to the ship after making some purchases.[16] Nabíl managed to convince the guard to let his friend into the prison. Inside, Nabíl was told about Bahá'u'lláh's presence in the ship and the two caught up with each other, explaining what they had recently encountered in the path of God.

That day was a Thursday and the next day all the public offices were closed, as Friday is the day of rest in Muslim countries, so Nabíl could not send a message to Bahá'u'lláh on the ship.

Therefore it was decided that the next morning Nabíl and Fáris, the other prisoner, would send their own messages to Bahá'u'lláh. Fáris was a Protestant physician who was converted to the Faith by Nabíl in prison. He is believed to be the first Christian to convert to the Bahá'í Faith. The message was going to be delivered by Constantine, a Christian watchmaker. According to Nabíl, Constantine,

> ... went out [rowing] in the morning. We were looking from the roof-top. We first heard the signal, and then the noise of the movement of the ship, and were perplexed, lest he had not made it. Then the ship stopped, and started again after a quarter of an hour. We were on tenterhooks, when suddenly Constantine arrived. He handed me an envelope and a package in

a handkerchief, and exclaimed, 'By God! I saw the Father of Christ.' Fáris, the physician, kissed his eyes and said, 'Our lot was the fire of separation, yours was the bounty of gazing upon the Beloved of the World.' In answer to our petitions, there was a Tablet, in the script of Revelation, a Letter from the Most Great Branch, and a paper filled by almond *nuql* [a sweet] sent by the Purest Branch [Mírzá Mihdí]. In the Tablet, Fáris, the physician, had been particularly honoured. One of the attendants had written: 'Several times I have witnessed evidences of power which I can never forget. And so it was today. The ship was on the move, when we saw a boat far away. The captain stopped the ship, and this young watch-maker [Constantine] reached us, and called aloud my name. We went to him and he gave us your envelope. All eyes were on us and we are exiles. Yet no one questioned the action of the captain.[17]

Interestingly, Bahíyyih Khánum many years later recalled that, to their amazement, Nabíl and Fáris, both in chains, were able to see 'Bahá'u'lláh and the Master standing amongst the friends on the deck of our boat.'[18]

While the ship was anchored in Alexandria, Bahá'u'lláh received a number of Persian visitors who paid their respects to Him. Although His passage through that port was unknown to all, it might have happened that some Persians travelling on the same ship from Gallipoli to Alexandria had spread the news of His presence among their local community.

Such was the stress the exiles suffered, particularly by the rumours of being separated, that on leaving the harbour at Alexandria en route to Haifa,

> One friend, in his dire distress, jumped into the sea, but was saved.
>
> Bahá'u'lláh and the Master cheered us. 'Why did you jump into the sea? Did you wish to give a banquet to the fishes?' asked Bahá'u'lláh.[19]

The ship's itinerary from Alexandria to Haifa included brief stops in Port Said in Egypt and Jaffa in Palestine. In the words of Bahíyyih Khánum:

> There was no place in which we could lie down in that vessel. There were also some Tartar passengers in the boat. To be near them was very uncomfortable; they were dirty beyond description.
>
> Our lack of food had reduced us to a seriously weak state of health.[20]

At Port Said, on the Suez Canal, the ship arrived the next morning, anchoring during the day and leaving at night. The steamship then proceeded, making another brief stop at Jaffa, a port located next to the present Tel Aviv, on southwest Asia, arriving there by sunset of the next day. From Jaffa the vessel continued to Haifa, which was reached the following morning. The Divine Mariner, as Bahá'u'lláh had earlier referred to Himself, disembarked the steamship at Haifa onto a small boat, and was subsequently taken to 'Akká in a sailing vessel. Bahíyyih Khánum recalled:

> After a voyage of about two days we were landed at Haifa, in Syria. All were sick, from hunger or eating improper food. I myself was a healthy woman up to the time of taking this voyage; since then I have never been well.
>
> We remained one day in the prison at Haifa, the men in chains . . .[21]

Exhausted after an 11-day sea journey on three different vessels, the exiles arrived from Haifa in 'Akká on a sailing boat on the late afternoon of 31 August 1868, only to be received and taken immediately by 30 soldiers to the local barracks. It was just five weeks after the Sultan had signed the terrible decree of exile in Constantinople that this historical trip touching three continents concluded. Nineteen days had passed since they had left Adrianople in haste.

The extraordinary spiritual significance of the sea voyage from Gallipoli to 'Akká' is described eloquently by the Universal House of Justice:

Neither the migration of Abraham from Ur of the Chaldees to the region of Aleppo, nor the journey of Moses towards the Promised Land, nor the flight into Egypt of Mary and Joseph with the infant Jesus, nor yet the Hegira of Muḥammad can compare with the voyage made by God's Supreme Manifestation one hundred years ago from Gallipoli to the Most Great Prison. Bahá'u'lláh's voyage was forced upon Him by the two despots who were His chief adversaries in a determined attempt to extirpate once and for all His Cause, and the decree of His fourth banishment came when the tide of His prophetic utterance was in full flood. The proclamation of His Message to mankind had begun; the sun of His majesty had reached its zenith and, as attested by the devotion of His followers, the respect of the population and the esteem of officials and the representatives of foreign powers, His ascendancy had become manifest.[22]

6

The Disembarkation in 'Akká

It was a Monday afternoon when the exiles disembarked at 'Akká's sea gate, a medieval structure, 'a narrow portal under the muzzles of the heavy cannon guarding the harbour mouth'.[1] The exiles, plus the ten accompanying officers, had arrived in Haifa in the early morning on an Austrian Lloyd steamer from Alexandria after a journey of nearly 70 hours, a journey that today takes about an hour by plane. Interestingly, Moses' attempt by land took about 40 years nearly 35 centuries ago.

Although 'Akká was an important centre of population, its bay could not cope with large liners and therefore boats were used to take passengers from the ship to the dock at Haifa. On approaching Haifa, the authorities began making arrangements to separate Mírzá Yaḥyá and his dependents from the rest of the travellers for their transportation to Cyprus. Four devoted Baháʼís who were ordered by the Sultan to accompany Mírzá Yaḥyá to Cyprus became very distressed at their imminent separation from Baháʼuʼlláh, as did the other exiles. According to Shoghi Effendi:

> It was at the moment when Bahá'u'lláh had stepped into the boat which was to carry Him to the landing-stage in Haifa that 'Abdu'l-Ghaffár, one of the four companions condemned to share the exile of Mírzá Yaḥyá, and whose 'detachment, love and trust in God' Bahá'u'lláh had greatly praised, cast himself, in his despair, into the sea, shouting 'Yá Bahá'u'l-Abhá', and was subsequently rescued and resuscitated with the greatest difficulty, only to be forced by adamant officials to continue his voyage, with Mírzá Yaḥyá's party, to the destination originally appointed for him.[2]

According to Bahíyyih Khánum, upon their arrival in Haifa, 'we had to be carried ashore in chairs'.[3] After waiting in Haifa for a few hours, Bahá'u'lláh and His companions were taken to 'Akká on a sailing ship provided by the authorities.

To appreciate the complexities of the logistics of the journey by modern standards, consider that there were 67 exiles plus the government officials on the boat. If each had only one piece of old-fashioned luggage, it would require at least a large modern bus to accommodate them. The 16-kilometre sea journey took eight hours and was very arduous owing to the rough waters, a lack of wind to propel the vessel, a lack of provisions and a lack of shelter from the blistering summer sun. The exiles disembarked in 'Akká at about 4.00 p.m.[4]

As the vessel did not come ashore in the 'Akká bay, the exiles had to walk back and forth through the water to collect their large amount of luggage. Bahíyyih Khánum described the arrival of the exiles:

> The Governor ordered that the women be carried on the backs of the men. My brother ['Abdu'l-Bahá] was not willing that this should be done, and protested against it. He was one of the first to land, and procured a chair, in which, with the help of one of the believers, he carried the women ashore. The Blessed Perfection was not allowed to leave his boat until all his family had landed. When he had come ashore, the family were counted and taken to the army barracks, in which we were to be imprisoned. From the terrible sufferings and privations of the journey we were nearly all sick; worst of all, perhaps, the Blessed Perfection and myself.[5]

As mentioned above, Bahá'u'lláh was not allowed to disembark until all His family had done so[6] and irreverence to the Supreme Manifestation of God was shown at all times. One of the exiles described that upon stepping onto the soil they were then 'counted as if they were sheep'.[7]

At the 'Akká sea gate the exiles were met with a large

number of people demonstrating against their arrival. There were also many curious people among the mob who wanted to see the face of the 'God of the Persians', as Bahá'u'lláh was referred to. Frantically fanatical, the populace was openly not in favour of their arrival or of the government's decision to send the exiles to their city. The exiles had been described as a religion of heretics and evil people. 'There was a detachment of soldiers on shore drawn up in two lines. Between these lines the prisoners walked to the barracks,' Bahíyyih Khánum related.[8] There were orders to shoot anyone who tried to escape from the prison.

The population of 'Akká at the time was about five thousand people.[9] The Holy Family's first impressions of the city after disembarking are illustrative of the gloomy environment the exiles encountered as they walked among the hostile local population and through the tortuous and lugubrious streets. 'Abdu'l-Bahá recounted:

> As we entered the place we found the inhabitants of Acca, without exception, sickly looking people of sallow, yellow complexion, a good many unable to walk and hence strewn on the narrow streets. Even the soldiers and officers, who possessed privileges, looked ill. In fact, a number of the soldiers, that is, those who were ordered to guard us, were very sick and I began treating them at once.[10]

THE DISEMBARKATION IN ʿAKKÁ

According to Bahíyyih Khánum:

> When we landed in Akka all the people of the town came crowding about us, talking loudly in Arabic, which I understood. Some said that we were to be put in the dungeons and chained; others that we were to be thrown into the sea. The most horrible jests and jeers were hurled at us as we were marched through the streets to this dreadful prison.[11]

> There was a line of soldiers from the shore to the barracks. First the women were taken up and locked in a room. Then the men were treated likewise.[12]

The march of nearly one kilometre towards the barracks from the sea gate through the winding, dirty and narrow ʿAkká streets must have taken about half an hour, excluding a stop at the police station located at about a third of the way along. ʿAbdu'l-Bahá later recalled while walking past this police station with a pilgrim, 'They first wanted to confine us here, but we did not accept. Then they took us to the barracks.'[13] This suggests that the local authorities might not have been adequately prepared to host the large number of exiles.

Notwithstanding the distance, it must have been a difficult walk. The exiles were exhausted after their 19-day journey. They had to take their personal belongings with them and carry the children who were more tired, hungry and thirsty than the adults themselves. Not knowing where they were being taken that hot summer afternoon, the long walk must have seemed interminable until they finally saw the bleak walls of the citadel and, with their last ounce of energy, climbed the high steps leading to their final destination. As they traversed the city's centre, they were able to see the misery in the city and perhaps glimpse some of its landmarks such as the three main caravanserais (inns), a Christian monastery, the busy local market and the main mosque, before being confined for two years, two months and five days.

Sunset on that day was at about 6:30 p.m. and therefore there was not much daylight left as the exiles progressed through 'Akká. Watched by a beautiful, almost full moon, the procession towards the prison must have been in sections. No doubt some of the men remained at the wharf to help with the baggage, which should have been considerable given that there were 67 people in the group and each person must have had at least one large piece of luggage containing clothes and personal effects.

In a small Arab town such as 'Akká, marked by monotony and dullness, the convoy must have attracted the crowd's attention. The unusual group of Persian travellers coming with the 20-year-old Mírzá Mihdí included some as young as a suckling baby and others as old as a grandmother; many looked well-educated; they dressed in different costumes, spoke a foreign language and most likely, as Bahá'ís do, tried to be polite to the mob. Among them was Bahá'u'lláh, whose majestic figure no doubt captured the interest of everyone, not only for His aristocratic gait, His kingly demeanour and His magnetic personality but also because of the controversial statements that had been made about Him by a merciless government that only wanted to discredit Him and limit His influence. They all had been labelled criminals of the Ottoman Empire.

Interestingly, among the ignorant crowd there was a different type of onlooker who perceived Bahá'u'lláh's glory and divine radiance as He made His way to the barracks. Adib Taherzadeh relates the story of two insightful citizens:

> Yet among the crowd there were some endowed with a measure of spiritual perception. These, as they gazed upon the countenance of Bahá'u'lláh, were struck by His majesty and witnessed a glory they had never seen before. Among them was a certain Khalíl Aḥmad 'Abdú, a venerable old man who used to say to the inhabitants of 'Akká that he could see in the face of Bahá'u'lláh signs of greatness and of majesty and truthfulness. He often said that the people of 'Akká should rejoice and be thankful to God for having

ennobled their homeland by the footsteps of this great Personage. He prophesied that through Him the inhabitants would be blessed and prosper, and this of course literally came to pass.

Another man in the crowd watching the arrival of the exiles was known as 'Abdu'lláh Ṭuzih. He saw the radiance, the power, and the glory of Bahá'u'lláh's countenance and was drawn to Him. He later became a believer and his daughter (who was born on the same day that Bahá'u'lláh arrived in 'Akká) was some years later joined in wedlock with Husayn-i-Áshchí, a cook in Bahá'u'lláh's household and one of His devoted servants.[14]

There were certainly those in town who held the belief that the Promised One would come to 'Akká. An old religious 'Akká shaykh had observed in 1850 to a father and his son that

> Unto this city of 'Akká will come one day the 'Great One'. He will abide in a high house with many, many steps. His sustenance will be provided by the Government (i.e., a prisoner). Now thou wilt be here, in this city, when He cometh. I and thy father will have passed form this mortal world, but mark well what I now say unto thee:
>
> 'We charge thee to deliver the salutation of our hearts' devoted worship unto Him, mine and thy father's.'[15]

This child, Shaykh Maḥmúd, grew up in the town and eventually became a strong believer, as described in the next chapter, being much loved by the Blessed Beauty. Above all, the prophecy enunciated by Prophet Muhammad:

> All of them (the companions of the Qá'im[16]) shall be slain except One Who shall reach the plain of 'Akká, the Banquet-Hall of God.[17]

which was widely known, is indicative that despite its foul environment, 'Akká had been blessed more than its 'generation of vipers'[18] deserved.

The Hand of the Cause of God Abu'l-Qasim Faizi has described those tense initial moments as Bahá'u'lláh told the exiles that these were history-making times:

> The moment Bahá'u'lláh stepped into the citadel He stopped and made a remarkable pronouncement – remarks which will echo throughout eternity in the hearts of all the adherents of His Faith. He pointed out to all who accompanied Him to the Most Great Prison the exalted position they occupied. He reminded them that thereafter their lives would take another form and would have a deeper significance. Even a breath breathed in that atmosphere and a step taken along that path would be immortalized. He saw a broken branch near His feet. He looked at it and declared that

even that broken twig would be mentioned in East and West. Thus He demanded from his family and followers an unswerving rectitude of character and an unflinching devotion to the Cause of God, so that all their words and deeds would become worthy of eternity.[19]

The disembarkation took several hours, with 'Abdu'l-Bahá's managing the whole process so further tribulations could be minimized. Bahíyyih Khánum said that as the companions were settling in the barracks,

> . . . my brother had slipped out and gone down to assist in the landing of the remainder of our company, whom we had left in the boats. When the soldiers discovered that he had disappeared, they at once notified the Governor, who had search made for him and found him helping the others ashore . . . He had been away for hours, and our hearts had been filled with anxiety for his safety.[20]

The process of settling in a foreign land, in the environs of the biblical Mount Carmel, had just begun. Through the forces of divine destiny, such a humble arrival would, in a matter of decades, transform the exiles' abasement into the magnificence of the Bahá'í World Centre and its glorious institutions in the Holy

Land. As the Bible had prophesied, the Lord of Hosts had just arrived, 'like the roar of rushing waters,'[21] in 'Akká, the 'fortified city,'[22] through 'the gate facing east,'[23] a 'door of hope.'[24] The Psalms also foretold that this was Bahá'u'lláh's destination: 'This is my resting place forever; Here I will dwell, for I have desired it.'[25]

Alas, although all the prophecies suggested that Bahá'u'lláh came to the Holy Land to stay – and so He did until His passing in 1892 – Mírzá Mihdí had less than two years to live before his tragic death. For the remaining period of his life, this tender soul grew further as God's Purest Branch, loved and admired within that small Bahá'í community and living an arm's length from his beloved father under the strict regulations of their confinement.

These days, thousands of tourists from all over the world flood to see what remains of the solitary yet famous 'Akká sea gate in the city's southern wall. Its historic value has increased because, apart from the 'Akká landing, we do not have precise records of what transpired in the other ports along the Mediterranean Sea. A number of old buildings still stand adjacent to that historical spot as silent observers of the continuity of time, custodians of an event that God wants us to recall and never forget. Looking across the Mediterranean Sea and the sacred Holy Land plains, the sea gate watches both the West and the East, wishing them peace, and standing as a permanent reminder to tyrannical governments that religious oppression will never succeed in the long term.

The sea gate is now protected as part of a UNESCO World Heritage Site, guaranteeing that its structure will survive into the future so that succeeding generations can reflect on the significance of that afternoon on 31 August 1868 and the momentous events that followed.

7

Life in the Barracks

When Bahá'u'lláh and the other exiles arrived in 'Akká, Mírzá Mihdí was 20 years old. As all the exiles but two fell ill shortly after their arrival in the barracks,[1] Mírzá Mihdí might well have been one of them, as he had had a delicate constitution when he was a child.

We know that he was already accustomed to hardship through the life he had led before coming to the prison: at the age of four being left behind in Tehran when his family went to Baghdad and only rejoining them when he was 11, and undertaking the journeys of the exiles from Baghdad to Adrianople and from there to 'Akká. The stories that follow in this chapter reveal the severe hardships he suffered but also demonstrate how the spiritual endurance he developed through his difficult lifetime helped him to serve the friends in trying circumstances. It was his stamina that undoubtedly sustained him through the rigours in the remaining 22 months he had left to live.

When they arrived the Holy Family was initially accommodated on the ground floor of the barracks in solid-walled rooms that overlooked the sea. Later they were moved one level up to the first floor. The severe

MÍRZÁ MIHDÍ

and unsanitary conditions were felt right from the start. Bahíyyih Khánum, Mírzá Mihdí's sister, recalled:

Arrived at the barracks, it was proposed to put the Blessed Perfection and his family on the second floor, and he was sent up; but I fainted from exhaustion and was unable to ascend the stairs. (Here the narrator paused a moment, visibly trembling, and then continued.) Of my own experience perhaps this is the most awful. The horrible sufferings of the voyage had reduced me almost to the point of death. Upon that came the sea sickness . . .

Imagine, if you can, the overpowering impression made by all this upon the mind of a young girl, such as I was then. Can you wonder that I am serious, and that my life is different from those of my countrywomen? But this is digressing.

When we had entered the barracks the massive door was closed upon us and the great iron bolts thrown home. I cannot find words to describe the filth and stench of that vile place. We were nearly up to our ankles in mud in the room into which we were led. The damp, close air and the excretions of the soldiers combined to produce horrible odours. Then, being unable to bear more, I fainted. As I fainted, those about me caught me before I fell; but because of the mud and filth there was no place upon which I could be laid. On one side of the room was a man weaving

LIFE IN THE BARRACKS

a mat for the soldiers. One of our friends took this mat and I was placed upon it. Then they begged for water, but they could not get it. The soldiers would permit no one to go out. There was a pool of water on the dirt floor, in which the mat-maker had been moistening his rushes. Some of this water was dipped up and strained and put to my lips. I swallowed a little and revived; but the water was so foul that my stomach rejected it, and I fainted again. Then a little of this water was thrown into my face; and at length I revived sufficiently to go up-stairs.

Then came another time of heart-sickening suffering. The mothers who had babes at breast had no milk for them, for lack of food and drink, so the babes could not be pacified or quieted. The larger children were screaming for food and water, and could not sleep or be soothed. The women were fainting.

Under these conditions, my brother spent the first part of the night in passing about among the distressed people, trying to pacify them, and in appealing to the soldiers not to be so heartless as to allow women and children to suffer so. About midnight he succeeded in getting a message to the Governor. We were then sent a little water and some cooked rice; but the latter was so full of grit and smelled so badly that only the strongest stomach could retain it. The water the children drank; but the rice only the strongest could eat. Later on, some of our people in unpacking their goods found some pieces of the bread which had been brought from Gallipoli, and a little sugar. With these a dish was prepared for the Blessed Perfection, who was very ill. When it was taken to him, he said: 'I command you to take this to the children.' So it was given to them, and they were somewhat quieted.

The next morning conditions were no better; there was neither water nor food that could be eaten. My brother sent message after message to the Governor, appealing in behalf of the women and children. At length he sent us water and some prisoners' bread; but the latter was worse even than the rice – appearing and tasting as though earth had been mixed with the flour. My brother also succeeded in getting permission to send out a servant, guarded by four soldiers, to buy food. But before this permission was given, the Governor commanded the presence of my brother and told him that neither he nor any of our people – not even a child – was to leave the prison under any circumstances whatever, and that unless this was promised the servant would not be permitted to go out. Under the circumstances my brother was obliged to give this promise.

The servant selected was told that if he spoke to a man or woman except in bargaining for supplies, he would be spitted on the swords of the soldiers.

The servant procured some provisions; yet even thus we were still badly off for food, for we were all so poor that we could buy but little. So the Blessed Perfection requested that the prison allowance for our support should be commuted for money. The Governor consented, and gave to my father the amount allowed our family, and to my brother the amount allowed to the others. Then my father gave his own share and that of our family to my brother for the people, the whole being insufficient for them, saying: 'I will eat bread.' Thereafter, when the supply of provisions was insufficient and he learned of it, he would take only bread and water.[2]

Of that first night in the prison Bahíyyih Khánum said decades later, 'There was no furniture, only a few rugs, and we had no food except some fragments of bread.'[3] Bahá'u'lláh Himself remarked that 'all were deprived of either food or drink . . . They even begged for water, and were refused.'[4]

In the days that followed, the companions had to be content with a ration of three loaves of salty black bread each. Bahá'u'lláh was first placed in a completely empty cell but was later put into a room whose floor was covered with earth and whose ceiling was peeling off, with pieces continuously falling onto the floor.[5] With no bed, sleeping on a few mats laid on the cold stone slab floor must have been a torturous experience for Bahá'u'lláh. For three months He was not allowed to go to the public bath. The barber attending Him in the prison was not allowed to talk to Him and He was constantly watched by a guard.

'There was no communication whatever with the outside world. Each loaf of bread was cut open by the guard to see that it contained no message,' 'Abdu'l-Bahá once said.[6]

The day after the arrival of the exiles, government officials visited them and met Bahá'u'lláh; they were surprised by His majesty and elevated knowledge. According to one of the exiles, the Blessed Beauty 'spoke such words of knowledge and wisdom that, in that very first meeting, they [the government entourage] realized that here were people endowed with erudition, wisdom and rare understanding. One of them had said, there and then, that never before had such pure and sanctified souls set foot in 'Akká.'[7]

A few days after the exiles disembarked at 'Akká the governor came to inspect the barracks. His attitude towards 'Abdu'l-Bahá and the group of believers was authoritarian and rude. The governor arrogantly warned 'Abdu'l-Bahá during this first inspection of the barracks that any escape would be punished by depriving them of food. Later he changed his assumptions about the behaviour of the Bahá'ís to a more humane stance and instructed that the daily ration of three loaves of bread be changed to a small sum of money for each person. This allowed a group of four exiles, accompanied by guards, to go to the market each morning to buy food for everyone so that they could prepare their own meals.

According to 'Abdu'l-Bahá,

> When we arrived in Acca it was found there were not enough rooms in the barracks to imprison us separately, so they put us all in two rooms with no furniture at all. The court of the barracks had a most gloomy aspect. There were three or four fig trees on the branches of which several ominous owls screeched all night.[8]
>
> How disquieting is the hoot of an owl; how it saddens the heart.[9]

All the rooms opened onto a central space which was accessed through a single opening leading to an outer section, described thus:

> The outer section of this area included a verandah (above which was the skylight), a kitchen, latrines, a mezzanine, and a biruni – a room Baha'u'llah used for receiving visitors. The eastern side faced the courtyard with three open arches bounded by pairs of columns serving as balcony openings (now filled in). Other Baha'is lived elsewhere in the citadel.'[10]

Another source indicated that the kitchen was located opposite Bahá'u'lláh's room, although it is logical to suggest that rooms were rearranged more than once during their imprisonment as the exiles embarked on a process of refurbishing them, notwithstanding their limited means. The verandah area held wooden furniture in its central area, directly under the skylight, and was a rudimentary family living room. This was the place where Mírzá Mihdí's accident took place. To get to the roof in which the skylight was situated, he used to climb a narrow stairway on one side of the verandah area.

Eventually, some families and individuals were moved to other places within the barracks, around the courtyard and close to the Holy Family's compartments. For example, the family of Bahá'u'lláh's younger brother, Mírzá Muḥammad-Qulí, was moved to the ground floor of the block while Bahá'u'lláh and His own family remained on the first floor. Mírzá Mihdí's other uncle, Mírzá Músá, was allocated a room around the citadel courtyard.

So pervasive were the unhealthy conditions in the middle of that summer of 1868, with malaria, typhoid and dysentery widespread, that three of the exiles died, including two brothers, Áqá Muḥammad-Ismá'il and Áqá Muḥammad-Báqír, who died while embracing each other. Bahá'u'lláh later reproached 'Alí Páshá, the prime minister of the Ottoman Empire, for those excesses in His Lawḥ-i-Ra'ís (Tablet to the Chief), revealed in the late summer of 1868, soon after those deaths took place:

Most of Our companions now lie sick in this prison, and none knoweth what befell Us, except God, the Almighty, the All-Knowing. In the days following Our arrival, two of these servants hastened to the realms above. For an entire day the guards insisted that, until they were paid for the shrouds and burial, those blessed bodies could not be removed, although no one had requested any help from them. At that time we were devoid of earthly means, and pleaded that they leave the matter unto us and allow those present to carry the bodies, but they refused. Finally, a carpet was taken to the bazaar to be sold, and the sum obtained was delivered to the guards. Later, it was learned that they had merely dug a shallow grave into which they had placed both blessed bodies, although they had taken twice the amount required for shrouds and burial.[11]

Thus it was that the carpet that Bahá'u'lláh used to have at His feet was sold at a low price. The prison officials took the money for themselves and buried the bodies of the two unfortunate victims without a coffin, with only the clothes that covered them. It was not even allowed to bury them in the Muslim cemetery and they had to be laid to rest elsewhere. Around the same time another believer, Abu'l-Qásim, died of typhus in the citadel. According to 'Abdu'l-Bahá, 'The Blessed Beauty expressed approval of him and the friends, all of them, wept over his afflictions and mourned him.'[12]

The authorities refused to call for a doctor to see the exiles so 'Abdu'l-Bahá took on the task of looking after the ill, although once He became very sick Himself, an incident that made all the companions extremely anxious. The local maladies were unknown to the companions. As Bahá'u'lláh once said, 'Fever is a product of this land. Whoever comes here must have it.'[13] In this regard, in 1920 Bahíyyih Khánum described to a pilgrim her apprehensions about the local standard of hygiene when the ladies were allowed to go to the 'Akká public bath one day, escorted by soldiers:

> After about fifteen days the women asked permission to go to the public bath. Permission was given . . . Khanum said that she cried after she had returned from the bath. She feared they would all come to look like the other women they saw in the bath, yellow skinned and with big hard bellies. This appearance is caused by malaria.[14]

'Abdu'l-Bahá Himself recalled many years later how critical the situation was for families like that of the elderly 'Alí-'Askar, which numbered eleven members in the prison. According to the Master, 'the prison was a palace to him, and captivity a reason to rejoice':[15]

> I hurried to the corner of the barracks where he lived – the cell that was his shabby nest. He was lying there,

LIFE IN THE BARRACKS

running a high fever, out of his head. On his right side lay his wife, shaking and trembling with chills. To his left was his daughter, Fátimih, burning up with typhus. Beyond them his son, Ḥusayn-Áqá, was down with scarlet fever; he had forgotten how to speak Persian, and he kept crying out in Turkish, 'My insides are on fire!' At the father's feet lay the other daughter, deep in her sickness, and along the side of the wall was his brother, Mashhadí Fattaḥ, raving and delirious. In this condition, 'Alí-'Askar's lips were moving: he was returning thanks to God, and expressing joy.[16]

When the companions were allowed to go out, accompanied by soldiers, to buy their own food, 'Abdu'l-Bahá Himself used to wait at the prison door to check that they did not bring back foods that might endanger their health. The Master even went to the extreme of checking the friends' pockets as they returned from the market. Daily supplies were eventually provided by a local shop and the accounts were settled monthly.[17] As one of the few young men among the group, Mírzá Mihdí might well have been called upon to help carry the large volume of provisions. The food was cooked in the kitchen under strict hygienic conditions and distributed to the friends, who numbered about 70.

The Blessed Perfection revealed a short healing prayer to be used in the barracks and, fortunately, there were no further fatalities. The prayer reads:

In the Name of God, the Forgiver! Although this evil state in which I am, O my God, maketh me deserving of Thy wrath and punishment, Thy good-pleasure and Thy bounties demand Thy forgiveness to encompass Thy servants and Thy good favour to reach them. I ask Thee by Thy Name which Thou hast made the King of all names to protect me by Thy power and Thine Omnipotence from all calamity and all that is repugnant to Thee and all that is contrary to Thy Will. Thou art Supreme over all things.[18]

About 30 years after the incarceration of the Bahá'ís, Bahíyyih Khánum, Bahá'u'lláh's daughter, entitled by Him the 'Greatest Holy Leaf', recounted the horrific conditions the group of exiles endured during their nearly 800 days in the 'Akká barracks:

> When we were first brought to the barracks we had no knowledge as to the manner of life to which we were to be consigned. We feared that the Blessed Perfection, my brother, and perhaps others would be placed in dungeons and chained. The only information about it which we could obtain was that our sentence would be read on Friday – our arrival being early in the week. This uncertainty was an additional horror. When the sentence was read to us, we learned that it stated that we were political prisoners, nihilists, murderers, and thieves; that wherever we went,

LIFE IN THE BARRACKS

we corrupted the morals of the people; that we had leagued to overthrow the Ottoman Empire; that we could be given no leniency, and that the orders to keep us under bolt and bar must not be broken. It was because of this evil reputation, which had doubtless been given to the government by those who had reasons for desiring our destruction, and not from any want of humanity on the part of our jailors, who later became very kind and friendly to us, that we were subjected to such stern treatment and were given no more latitude or aid.

The season was summer (1868) and the temperature very high. All our people were huddled together on the damp earth floor of the barracks; with little water to drink, and that very bad, with no water with which to bathe, and scarcely enough for washing their faces. Typhoid fever and dysentery broke out among them. Every one in our company fell sick excepting my brother, my mother, an aunt, and two others of the believers. We were not allowed a physician; we could not procure medicine. My brother had in his baggage some quinine and bismuth. With these two drugs and his nursing, he brought us all through with the exception of four, who died. These were two months of such awful horror as words cannot picture. Imagine it, if you can. Some seventy men, women, and children packed together, hot summer weather, no proper food, bad water, the most offensive odours from purging and excretions, and a general attack of the terrible diseases of dysentery and typhoid.

There was no one with strength to be of any general service but my brother. He washed the patients, fed them, nursed them, watched with them. He took no rest. When at length he had brought the rest of us – the four who died excepted – through the crisis and we were out of danger, he was utterly exhausted and fell sick himself, as did also my mother and the three others who had theretofore been well. The others soon recovered, but Abbas Effendi ['Abdu'l-Bahá] was taken with dysentery, and long remained in a dangerous condition. By his heroic exertions he had won the regard of one of the officers, and when this man saw my brother in this state he went to the Governor and pleaded that Abbas Effendi might have a physician. This was permitted, and under the care of the physician my brother recovered.

For long after our departure from Adrianople none of the friends and followers of the Blessed Perfection in Persia knew our whereabouts. We were not permitted to send any letters. Great efforts were made to find us, and our friends finally traced us to Akka; but this whole city was then practically a prison from which strangers were carefully excluded, and they found it impossible to get into communication with us, or even to pass the city gate.

There was a Persian follower of the Bab ['Abdu'l-

Ahad] who some time before, having failed in his business at home, had emigrated to Akka. He had not dared to disclose his faith, and no one suspected it. The servant who marketed for us happened one day, as he went about the bazaar, to come to this man's shop; and though he was not allowed to speak with him, he seems to have known intuitively that he was a friend. So thereafter he made most of his purchases of provisions at his shop. Some of the Persian believers who had come to Akka, but who had been unable to enter the city, effected communication with this man and arranged with him to send a note to the Blessed Perfection. This the shopkeeper accomplished by concealing the note among some vegetables and giving them to the servant with such a look that the latter understood and afterwards searched for it. The note begged the Blessed Perfection to send out some word; but this seemed to be beyond our power.

The physician [Dr Boutros or Peter, a Greek doctor] who visited my brother, on seeing our condition, had so much sympathy with our distress, and became so fond of Abbas Effendi, that he asked him if there was not something which he could do for us. My brother begged him to take a message to the believers who were waiting to hear from the Blessed Perfection. He undertook to do so, and carried a tablet away in the lining of his hat. For two years this physician conveyed tablets and messages to and fro for us in this way.

MÍRZÁ MIHDÍ

After this first message had been transmitted from the Blessed Perfection, many believers came here from Persia and remained in the neighbourhood with the hope of effecting some communication with him, or at least of getting a glimpse of him. They would go to some prominent point where they could be seen from his window. Some of us, seeing them, would call my brother's attention to them, whereupon he would inform the Blessed Perfection and follow him to the window and wave his handkerchief.[19]

By the end of autumn the exiles had better adapted to the harsh environment while the guards had adopted a more benign attitude towards them. After all, they were people who constantly spoke of spiritual issues, lived a prayerful life, strived to be happy, chanted their devotions in beautiful tones, had the highest moral standards and showed love and compassion to one another, including to the guards themselves. Might not the barrack sentinels have wondered in their inmost being, 'How, then, could these prisoners be guilty of conspiring against the government and be enemies of God?' As related by Bahíyyih Khánum, '. . . after six months or a year, when they saw that not a soul ever tried to escape, they gave us greater freedom and the friends could go out in the bazaar to buy things, either followed by one soldier or none.'[20]

As indicated earlier, Mírzá Mihdí would help with

many tasks, mainly serving as Bahá'u'lláh's amanuensis, that is, as His personal secretary. The term itself means 'within reach of the hand' in Latin. Amanuenses usually had good calligraphy skills and were engaged in writing down what their masters said as well as making handwritten copies from those records. To be a member of Bahá'u'lláh's group of amanuenses was more than a job, it was an honour conferred on a believer. It meant one had won the confidence of Bahá'u'lláh to transcribe His words accurately, and that one had close physical association with Him, receiving direct instructions from the Manifestation of God on a regular basis and sharing some of the latest revelations with the friends to cheer their hearts. Certainly Mírzá Mihdí appreciated such an appointment and did his best to live up to the high standard required. Referring to the period the exiles spent in the barracks, his sister Bahíyyih Khánum once said:

> The Blessed Perfection passed his time in his room, writing tablets or rather dictating them to my younger brother [Mírzá Mihdí], who was a rapid penman. Abbas Effendi ['Abdu'l-Bahá] would copy them and send them out by the physician [Dr Boutros, in order to be taken out of the prison].
>
> It was usual to carry on this work during the evening.[21]

Although we do not have detailed records about how the exiles spent their days, it is easy to imagine that once the restrictions were ameliorated and the exiles were assigned to other empty rooms within the citadel, they formed an unusual neighbourhood around the courtyard. It was a place where the children could run up and down, the families could meet and talk during the day, where people could take a stroll and get some fresh air and sunlight or do a bit of exercise away from their grim apartments – but always under the strict vigilance of the guards.

During His travels in the United States in 1912 'Abdu'l-Bahá spoke about aspects of His living conditions in the 'Akká barracks:

> . . . I noticed that my own presence in that crowded room was another source of torture to all of them. This was due to the fact that parents and children were suppressing and restraining themselves by trying to be quiet and polite in my presence. So, in order to give them freedom, I accepted the morgue of the barracks, because that was the only room available, and I lived in it for about two years.[22]

At the entrance of the barracks there was a morgue. It was a horrible looking room, yet I lived there two years in the utmost happiness. Up to that period I had not had time to read the Koran from first to last, but then I had ample time and used to read this Holy Book with fervour and enthusiasm. Going over the incidents and events of the lives of former Prophets, and finding how parallel they were with ours, I was consoled and encouraged. I would read for instance, the following verse:

'How thoughtless are the people! Whenever a Prophet is sent to them, they either ridicule him or persecute him.' And then I would read this verse: 'Verily, Our Host is victorious over them.' I was very happy all the time, because I was a free man. Shut off in that room, my spirit travelled throughout the immensity of space.

The soul of man must be happy no matter where he is. One must attain to that condition of inward beatitude and peace – then outward circumstances will not alter his spiritual calmness and joyousness. No one can imagine a worse place than the barracks of Acca.[23]

While emphasizing the importance of music in the Bahá'í Faith, 'Abdu'l-Bahá recalled that

Bahá'u'lláh, when He first came to the barracks (Acca) repeated this statement: 'If among the immediate followers there had been those who could have played some musical instrument, i.e., flute or harp, or could have sung, it would have charmed every one.'[24]

MÍRZÁ MIHDÍ

Adib Taherzadeh in his book *The Revelation of Bahá'u'lláh* tells us about the resilient attitude shown by the exiles living in the barracks:

> There is a Tablet revealed by Bahá'u'lláh in the barracks on the ninth day of the Festival of Riḍván. It was probably revealed during Riḍván 1869, the first of the two Riḍván Festivals that He celebrated in the prison, for in it He mentions the names of several believers who had tried to enter 'Akká and been stopped by the authorities.
>
> In this Tablet Bahá'u'lláh describes how on that day He was invited by one of the believers in the prison to honour his room with His presence and attend the celebration of that great Festival. His companions on that day were truly intoxicated with the wine of His presence. The believer who had invited Bahá'u'lláh entertained Him with the best food he could provide. Bahá'u'lláh refers to this and states that other believers had invited Him to their rooms during the Riḍván period also. Each according to his capacity had provided some food and some had nothing to entertain Him with except a cup of tea.[25]

Reflecting on the spiritual attributes of enduring such tests in the path of God with joy and acceptance, Myron Phelps remarks:

LIFE IN THE BARRACKS

Notwithstanding this interminable catalogue of the extreme and almost incredible sufferings and privations which this heroic band of men and women have endured – more terrible than many martyrdoms – there is not a trace of resentment or bitterness to be observed amongst them. One would suppose that they were the most fortunate of the people among whom they live, as, indeed, they do certainly consider themselves, in that they have always been permitted to live near their beloved Lord, beside which they count their sufferings as nothing.[26]

Initially forbidden to step out of those cold and damp quarters, the holy prisoners could only observe from a distance the noisy populace engaged in their daily pursuits and listen to the endless waves calling from the Mediterranean Sea lying metres below. The daily monotony was broken only by the reverberating calls to prayer chanted loudly from the nearby mosque throughout each day. We can imagine in such a restricted space mothers nursing babies, playful children entertained with rudimentary toys, youth endlessly concerned about their future and adults in daily sombre conversations wondering what was going to happen to them and their families next. We can even visualise Mírzá Mihdí, 'in the habit of going onto the roof of the barracks for prayers ... pacing in a state of prayer, attracted to the Kingdom of Abhá, with his head turned upwards . . .'[27] And we can also visualize all the exiles, like the Bábís before them, including Bahá'u'lláh, thrown together into the pestilential Síyáh-Chál of Tehran, praying fervently to ease their burdened hearts, in their daily communions chanting with fervour the divine verses, praising their Lord and manifesting their submission to His will, whatever it might be.

There were about seven mothers within the group, looking after their children and engaged in domestic chores. Cooking was a task shared by men and women alike, with all the exiles huddled together for the meals. Cooking for people with different dietary requirements owing to their varied acquired maladies must have been a challenge for the cooks. Among them, the young Ḥusayn was an experienced and reliable cook, used to preparing meals for a large group since the Adrianople days. In addition, cooking for about 70 people twice a day on a wood fire and without proper kitchen utensils must have been difficult. Soup apparently helped to preserve and improve the health of the companions, and soup-making was a skill that 'Abdu'l-Bahá mastered. In one of His talks in the West He laughingly said, 'I used to make broth for the people and as I had much practice, I made good broth.'[28]

Clearing the rooms of the large amount of dust that a dirty city such as 'Akká produces must have been a formidable task. Most likely the youth such as Mírzá Mihdí helped the group with the household tasks. Men were in charge of buying food from the local market on a daily basis, as there were no refrigeration facilities typical of this modern age. Other heavy duties included cleaning the latrines, doing maintenance jobs and carrying water from outside and up the stairs to the upper rooms. Such was the service undertaken by Aẓím-i-Tafrishí, who 'since he was the family water carrier', as 'Abdu'l-Bahá has attested, 'had the honour of coming into Bahá'u'lláh's presence every day'.[29] Because the water in the barracks was not drinkable, a better supply had to be brought from a well ten minutes' walk away from the prison. Aẓím carried skins of water over his shoulders, making numerous trips.

Ṭúbá Khánum, talking about her grandmother Navváb, Mírzá Mihdí's mother, shed more light on the harsh conditions in the barracks:

> As no laundress was allowed to come whilst we were all in the barrack prison at 'Akká, she did much of the washing and cooking, helped always by my dear aunt Khánum.
>
> The only servant they had, a negress, had neither time nor strength to do all that was needed. My grandmother and Khánum, then quite young, did much of the hard work, so that this servant should not be overtired.

They also made and mended the garments of the family, a formidable undertaking.[30]

The elderly no doubt spent time passing on their knowledge to the younger generation, teaching them the arts of reading and writing, the memorization and study of the Word of God, literature and poetry, and, in particular, teaching them calligraphy, a craft very much appreciated in those times and certainly a very useful one for those helping in the daily transcription and copying of the Holy Tablets. The prison-block, although cut off from the rest of the Bahá'í world, had become the spiritual and administrative centre of the Cause of God in those years by virtue of the presence and authority the Blessed Beauty. In all of the above roles, 'Abdu'l-Bahá's natural leadership was decisive in dealing with internal issues and external affairs. According to Adib Taherzadeh, 'At one stage 'Abdu'l-Bahá engaged a certain Egyptian by the name of Ḥájí 'Alíy-i-Misrí to come to the barracks and teach the prisoners the art of making rush mats.'[31]

Dealing with Bahá'u'lláh's correspondence as His amanuensis meant that Mírzá Mihdí had personal encounters with brilliant souls such as Shaykh Salmán, the Bahá'í who acted as a courier between Iran and the Holy Land every year. 'Abdu'l-Bahá said of him that 'From the dawn of history until the present day, there has never been a messenger so worthy of trust; there has never been a courier to compare with Salmán'.³² We know that by the second year of the exiles' imprisonment the correspondence between the Blessed Beauty and the Persian believers had grown so much that Shaykh Salmán was detained in Aleppo, Syria, carrying about 300 petitions addressed to Bahá'u'lláh.³³ The officer who arrested him described the messages as having been composed with spirituality and style and conveying supplications such as:

> O God! keep me safe from the evil of selfish and carnal desires, give me constancy, make me steadfast in Thy love, bestow on me the bounty of servitude, confirm me in service to Thy Cause, make me free of all else save Thee, confirm us that we may serve the people of all the world, kiss the hand of the executioner and hands clapping, feet dancing, hurry to the scaffold.³⁴

Although there is no written evidence regarding this, it is very likely that the exiles had established their own daily routines to survive the incarceration and let life take its course. We can visualize a small school to teach the children reading, writing and basic arithmetic. We know, for example, that Navváb and Mírzá Músá taught Mírzá Mihdí and his siblings. Bahá'u'lláh remained in His cell most of the time but it is reported that He met visitors in another room, although such interviews were infrequent because He did not want to give the impression of disobeying the government ruling associated with the edict exiling Him.

Under such backbreaking circumstances and poor hygiene only the fittest could survive. According to 'Abdu'l-Bahá, eight of the ten gaolers guarding the exiles fell sick and died. When in 1870 a group of 86 Bulgarian political prisoners were brought to the 'Akká barracks a third of them perished owing to the harsh environment. Nevertheless, during those interminable days and nights, when time seemed to stop and there was nowhere to go, the Bahá'í exiles were engaged in God's remembrance and rendered praise to the Divine Will.

One of the believers who virtually died in the barracks and was resurrected by Bahá'u'lláh was Mírzá Ja'far. 'Abdu'l-Bahá once told his story:

> At the time when we were in the barracks he [Mírzá Ja'far] fell dangerously ill and was confined to his bed. He suffered many complications, until finally the doctor gave him up and would visit him no more. Then the sick man breathed his last. Mírzá Áqá Ján ran to Bahá'u'lláh, with word of the death. Not only had the patient ceased to breathe, but his body was already going limp. His family were gathered about him, mourning him, shedding bitter tears. The Blessed Beauty said, 'Go; chant the prayer of Yá Sháfí – O Thou, the Healer – and Mírzá Ja'far will come alive. Very

rapidly, he will be as well as ever.' I reached his bedside. His body was cold and all the signs of death were present. Slowly, he began to stir; soon he could move his limbs, and before an hour had passed he lifted his head, sat up, and proceeded to laugh and tell jokes.[35]

Notwithstanding the gloomy circumstances surrounding the companions' lives, in several Tablets revealed in the barracks the Blessed Beauty had said, 'Do not grieve. These doors will be opened and I will leave the city and go to the country'; and 'ere long these doors will be open and My Tent will be pitched outside the walls.'[36]

At times, as 'Abdu'l-Bahá once recalled during His historic trip to the United States in 1912, the atmosphere was lightened by exchanging funny stories among the imprisoned Bahá'ís to make their tribulations easier. A witness remembered what the Master said on that occasion:

> It is good to laugh. Laughter is a spiritual relaxation. When they were in prison, He said, and under the utmost deprivation and difficulties, each of them at the close of the day would relate the most ludicrous event which had happened. Sometimes it was a little difficult to find one but always they would laugh until the tears would roll down their cheeks. Happiness, He said, is never dependent upon material surroundings,

otherwise how sad those years would have been. As it was they were always in the utmost state of joy and happiness.[37]

A believer also recalled 'Abdu'l-Bahá saying that 'during the most dangerous and trying times of His imprisonment Bahá'u'lláh would ask each member of the family to relate the most amusing incident or story they had experienced or heard that day. After the tale had been told, they would all roar with laughter.'[38]

The Master once spoke of the time when He was taken to court to be read the official edict of imprisonment, demonstrating His elevated wisdom and humour in those critical times:

> When we first arrived in 'Akká and entered the army barracks, the government authorities informed us one day that an individual representing Bahá'u'lláh should go and hear the Sultan's farmán. The Blessed Beauty sent me to Government House as His representative. First they put me where the guilty ones are placed. Then the public speaker went behind a podium and read the royal decree, which was in Turkish. In essence, it said that the family of Bahá'u'lláh would be imprisoned in 'Akká for ever and that they would have not the right to leave the city. After hearing this edict I laughed. Those present were quite surprised and asked me, 'Why do you laugh?' I said, 'This passage

has no meaning. If we were to remain in the city forever, we must also live forever. But we are not going to live eternally.'[39]

On another occasion 'Abdu'l-Bahá said:

Freedom is not a matter of place, but of condition. I was happy in that prison, for those days were passed in the path of service.

To me prison was freedom.

Troubles are a rest to me.

Death is life.

To be despised is honour.

Therefore, was I full of happiness all through that prison time.

When one is released from the prison of self, that is, indeed, freedom! For self is the greatest prison.

When this release takes place, one can never be imprisoned. Unless one accepts dire vicissitudes, not with dull resignation, but with radiant acquiescence, one cannot attain this freedom.[40]

Mírzá Mihdí was very close to 'Abdu'l-Bahá because, among many other reasons, they were nearer to each other in age than they were to others at the barracks. It is noteworthy that the relationship between Bahá'u'lláh and His family was marked by the family's sense of profound reverence, requiring them to respect the distance between the exalted position of the Manifestation of God and His believers, including His close relatives. In maintaining such a practice Bahíyyih Khánum explained:

> I should perhaps here say a word about our relations, in the family, to the Blessed Perfection. After his declaration we all regarded him as one far above us, and tacitly gave him a corresponding position in our demeanour towards him. He was never called upon to consider, or take part in, any worldly matters. We felt no claim upon him because of family relationship - no more than that of his other followers. When we had but two rooms for all, one was set apart for him. The best of everything was always given to him, he would take it and then return it to us and do without. He slept upon the floor because his people had no beds, although he would have been furnished one had he wished it.[41]

Outside the prison walls the Persian pilgrims could do little else but watch and prayfully circumambulate the fortress to mitigate their anxiety, hapless as they were and unable to render any assistance, while the Bahá'í community in Iran, months away by road, waited in anguish.

The souls in the prison saw their confinement as the realization of a major objective of Bahá'u'lláh:

The Ancient Beauty hath consented to be bound with chains that mankind may be released from its bondage, and hath accepted to be made a prisoner within this most mighty Stronghold that the whole world may attain unto true liberty. He hath drained to its dregs the cup of sorrow, that all the peoples of the earth may attain unto abiding joy, and be filled with gladness. This is of the mercy of your Lord, the Compassionate, the Most Merciful. We have accepted to be abased, O believers in the Unity of God, that ye may be exalted, and have suffered manifold afflictions, that ye might prosper and flourish. He Who hath come to build anew the whole world, behold, how they that have joined partners with God have forced Him to dwell within the most desolate of cities![42]

The Purest Branch lived up to the honour of sharing his father's imprisonment in the military barracks of 'Akká. Such spiritual privilege helped him to sustain the hardships that he and his family were going through. Because he understood Bahá'u'lláh's true station, Mírzá Mihdí translated that understanding into love and compassion for the friends, alleviating their pain and misfortunes for the 22 months that he stayed with them. Service to Bahá'u'lláh was indeed the same as Mírzá Mihdí's service to His loved ones – and was his own source of joy and happiness.

Even before he dwelt in a dreadful fortress and was

touched by death, that precious being was residing in a heavenly palace, living the life of a prisoner yet abiding in the very paradise, moving on a plane suspended between heaven and earth, well befitted to wear one day the immortal crown of martyrdom.

8
The First Bahá'í Pilgrims

We may assume that the Bahá'ís were very concerned about the conditions under which Bahá'u'lláh and His family were confined. When these believers, both in Iran and Iraq, learned of Bahá'u'lláh's imminent exile from Adrianople to a destination uncertain and insecure, they became deeply distressed. According to Shoghi Effendi:

> Such was the isolation imposed upon them that the Bahá'ís of Persia, perturbed by the rumours set afloat by the Azalís of Iṣfáhán that Bahá'u'lláh had been drowned, induced the British Telegraph office in Julfá to ascertain on their behalf the truth of the matter.[1]

Azalís were the followers of Mírzá Yaḥyá, the sinister half-brother of Bahá'u'lláh and uncle to Mírzá Mihdí. A number of them had been included in the decree that exiled Bahá'u'lláh and His companions and sent them to 'Akká. However, they asked to be accommodated elsewhere and were housed in a room over the city gates and Liman gaol. From such a strategic position they could easily monitor the gate into the city and note the arrival of Bahá'ís in the prison-city after a journey of nearly five months. As soon as they identified a believer, the Azalís would quickly reveal his identity to the authorities, which was how several Bahá'ís were arrested and expelled from the city.

No doubt the pilgrims were very concerned about the conditions inside the prison. Being unable to glimpse beyond those bleak and dilapidated walls, the pilgrims, judging from the appearance of these external walls, must have suspected that the living conditions inside were very depressing for Bahá'u'lláh and the exiles, particularly for those of a delicate constitution, such as Mírzá Mihdí. While their suspicions were correct regarding the material environment inside the prison, those fortunate enough to step into the barracks found a lively community of souls revolving like a celestial court around the King of Kings. Holiness and saintliness infused the atmosphere, bringing forth the finest spiritual resources of each believer. No wonder 'Abdu'l-Bahá wrote that 'During that long stay in the prison they were never neglectful of duty, never at fault. They were constantly joyful, for they had drunk deep of the holy cup . . .'[2] 'The prison changed into a palace, the jail itself became a Garden of Eden.'[3]

For instance, in describing the elevated condition of the believers, the Master noted that for one of the exiles 'The Prison was a garden of roses to him, and his narrow cell a wide and fragrant place,'[4] while another companion was 'always in a certain corner of the prison, silently meditating, occupied with the remembrance of God; at all times spiritually alert and mindful, in a state of supplication'.[5]

What, one might ask, could be more joyous than living in close contact with, metres away from, the Supreme Manifestation of God and gazing frequently on His blessed countenance? – 'achieving that greatest of all distinctions, to be in prison with the Blessed Beauty', as 'Abdu'l-Bahá wrote.[6] For instance, one believer wrote poems in praise of the Blessed Beauty, such as these beautiful lines:

> A hundred hearts Thy curling locks ensnare,
> And it rains hearts when Thou dost toss Thy hair.[7]

'Abdu'l-Bahá also recounted many years later what He went through with His younger brother Mírzá Mihdí:

> When we arrived at 'Akká, we were in a state of abject misery, each and every one of us endured hardship and calamity. Yet we experienced a joy and happiness that was far beyond description. At one time, at least 80 of us were crowded into but a few cells of that fortress-prison and all contracted fever to such a degree that no one except Áqá-Ridá and myself were able to move. We were night and day engaged in tending the sick, administering medicine, and so on. By the way,

my own room was very cold and damp, and the floor was made of stone. This room was in fact a morgue. Still under conditions such as these, we were under the blessings of Bahá'u'lláh and were so happy that we would consider any hardship a comfort.[8]

The power attracting these pilgrims to the Holy Land was not only Bahá'u'lláh's magnetic personality and the demonstration of His supreme leadership of the Bábí community over the previous two decades but also the blessings promised by the Báb upon those reaching the presence of 'Him Whom God will make manifest'. In the Bayán, the Báb had written:

> There is no paradise more wondrous for any soul than to be exposed to God's Manifestation in His Day, to hear His verses and believe in them, to attain His presence, which is naught but the presence of God, to sail upon the sea of the heavenly kingdom of His good-pleasure, and to partake of the choice fruits of the paradise of His divine Oneness.[9]

Soon, more Persian pilgrims began to flow into 'Akká. Many made the long overland journey enduring hardships, danger and risks. According to Moojan Momen:

> In the atmosphere of fear and suspicion in which most of the Iranian Bahá'ís lived, it was something of

a problem for those wishing to visit Akka to explain their prolonged absence (usually for several months) to their neighbours and acquaintances. This problem was solved by using the annual Hajj pilgrimage as a cover for visiting 'Akká. For Bahá'ís living in the south of Iran, the easiest route was to join the Hajj traffic to the Hejaz by sea from Bushehr to Jeddah; to perform the rites of pilgrimage and then join the Damascus caravan of pilgrims leaving the Hejaz. This took them to within easy reach of 'Akká. Bahá'ís from the north-west of Iran would use the overland route via Mosul and Aleppo.

The return journey for all travellers would usually be through Beirut, Aleppo and Mosul.[10]

These pilgrims were prevented from reaching the cell of Bahá'u'lláh itself and had to stand at one of the fortress counterscarps, trying for hours to see the figure of their Beloved. 'Abdu'l-Bahá would then advise the Blessed Beauty of their presence and together would go to a particular window where Bahá'u'lláh would extend His hand through and wave a handkerchief in a gesture of affection and appreciation of the efforts of His troubled disciples.[11] After a glimpse of their Beloved – some having better fortune than others – many of the pilgrims undertook the return journey, treasuring in their hearts that moving experience and sharing it with the worried friends in Iran, the cradle of the Faith. Others were left to roam the area, making their home on Mount Carmel and elsewhere. Some remained and settled in the neighbourhood, oblivious of their past and relatives, and rendering whatever service they could perform, finally laying down their bones to rest in the Holy Land.

Like the Báb, who stood 'concealed at the point of ice amidst the ocean of fire',[12] Bahá'u'lláh's glory was an energizing sun, sustaining life for all those around Him to the extent that the difficulties of prison itself became a magical world of light and blessings. The pilgrims felt that enchanting power as soon as they stepped near, and they left completely transformed into elevated beings, wholly liberated from the anchors fixing them to this terrestrial plain. Attached to that sacred spot, longing to come back once again, these pilgrims, like satellites attracted by a divine spiritual gravity, would circumambulate the prison as a consolation and an act of worship, reluctant to undertake the journey back to Iran.

No degree of poverty, no family, danger, sickness or other material concern was strong enough to draw them away from the Manifestation of God, who radiated power like a colossal engine from His modest but heavenly cell. The centre of their universe had changed forever and so their reason to live. The world around them became another world and they would never be the same again; they had attained another plane of existence. The dearest wish of their lives had been granted and, in such consummation, they were totally intoxicated by the love of the Beloved. Upon their eventual return to Iran, the pilgrims would ignite their local communities, share their unique experiences and engage tirelessly in propagating the new Gospel, some of them obtaining the peerless crown of martyrdom.

The first of the pilgrims to meet Bahá'u'lláh within the prison walls was Abu'l-Ḥasan-i-Ardikání, who was able to see Him only in the public bath at a carefully arranged meeting. He was asked not to give any sign of being a Bahá'í or to approach Bahá'u'lláh. It is said that when his eyes fell upon his Lord, he fell to the ground unconscious, overcome by emotion. Later, the Blessed Beauty revealed a special Tablet for him:

> Thou art the first one to attain the divine presence in His mighty, His Most Great Prison. Take heed lest what thou hast heard from the tongue of thy Lord, the Potent, the Powerful, be obliterated from thy heart. Make thou mention of Him all the time and call to mind the days when thou didst enter the most desolate of the cities until thou didst present thyself before the face of thy Lord, the Ruler of the Day of Judgement, and achieved that which is ordained for thee in His Preserved Tablet.[13]

That the danger of being discovered created tension is obvious. A married couple who wanted to determine whether Bahá'u'lláh was indeed imprisoned in 'Akká left Iran for the prison-city. There, cautiously, they contacted 'Abdu'l-Ahad, who, as mentioned earlier, had opened a small business in 'Akká. In order to keep their Bahá'í identity secret, the believers were hidden among boxes at the shop so as to avoid detection. None of the prisoners – neither Bahá'u'lláh nor Mírzá Mihdí nor even 'Abdu'l-Bahá – had been able to contact 'Abdu'l-Ahad directly for six months after their arrival in 'Akká, so great was the danger of the authorities discovering he was a Bahá'í.

Bahá'u'lláh, with much difficulty, learned of the presence of the married couple but instructed them to return to Iran. They were to remain only three days in the citadel before making the return journey. Although disappointed at not being able to see the face of the Blessed Perfection, they shared with the Bahá'í community the good news that their Lord was alive in the Holy Land.

Another arrival was Nabíl-i-A'ẓam, the humble shepherd who eventually became the great historian of the Bahá'í Faith. With great sorrow he was resigned to the prisoners' fate and went to see with sadness and helplessness the window of Bahá'u'lláh's cell from the citadel walls.

As explained above, among the exiles who had come to 'Akká were a few Covenant-breakers, the followers of Mírzá Yaḥyá. Although subject to the edict of exile, they were, through malicious conversations with local authorities, released of its rigours on condition that they report to the governor the presence of any Bahá'í visitor. The Covenant-breakers had been housed at the city gate, the only position from which their role as spies was possible. As they were familiar with the followers of Bahá'u'lláh, after his arrival Nabíl was soon identified.

'He is a Persian,' the Covenant-breakers told the authorities. 'He is not, as he seems, a man of Bukhárá [a city in Uzbekistan]. He has come here to seek for news of Bahá'u'lláh.'[14] Nabíl was thus intercepted and interrogated. He explained that the reason for his stay was to make some purchases but his argument was not accepted and he was expelled from the city.

Overwhelmed with grief, Nabíl wandered through the countryside around Galilee, Safad, Hebron, Nazareth and Haifa before making his home in a cave on Mount Carmel, not far from 'Akká. There Nabíl lived completely separate from everything, praying and communing with his Lord, longing for the time of their meeting. It is said that one day as he was walking on the walls surrounding the fort, Nabíl suddenly noticed Bahá'u'lláh who through the prison windows was extending His hand and expressing His love to him. That same day Nabíl was honoured with a prayer specially revealed to him. Eventually Nabíl was summoned to 'Akká and stayed 81 days, from 21 March to 9 June 1870, inside the citadel. Surely Mírzá Mihdí enjoyed his companionship and partook of Nabíl's broad, eye-witness knowledge of the history of his father's Faith.

The year before, in early 1869, the immortal youth of 17 years, Badíʿ, carrying the skins of a water-carrier, had slipped into the city of ʿAkká without being detected. Not knowing anyone to ask for more information and in fear of being identified, Badíʿ wandered through the tortuous ʿAkká streets looking for clues that would lead him to the Baháʾí exiles. He headed to the mosque to pray and release the burdens of his heart when suddenly, at sunset, he saw ʿAbduʾl-Bahá and a group of Baháʾís. Badíʿ recognized them and, without anyone noticing, gave the Master a piece of paper, identifying himself in a two-line poem as a believer. The same night, through the efforts of ʿAbduʾl-Bahá, Badíʿ, dressed as a water-carrier bearing the tools of his trade, was introduced into the barracks and attained Baháʾuʾlláh's presence.

The incomparable blessing of having an interview with the Manifestation of God was given to Badíʿ on two occasions. It was in the course of these two private interviews that Baháʾuʾlláh gave to this 17-year-old youth his new name, Badíʿ, literally, 'Unique' or 'Wonderful' in Arabic. The Blessed Perfection related that He created this boy's spirit for a second time: 'We took a handful of dust, mixed it with the waters of might and power and breathed into it the spirit of assurance.'[15]

During a meeting at which several believers were present, Bahá'u'lláh took the epistle He had written for the Persian monarch and asked, 'Who is the one who will carry this to the Shah of Persia?' Almost instinctively Badí' leapt from his seat and, bowing to the Messenger of God, said, 'I will carry this Tablet.' The Blessed Beauty once more repeated the question and the young pilgrim again begged for this great honour. For the third time the same question was asked and Badí' requested once again to be considered for the dangerous mission that would most likely lead to his martyrdom.[16]

Bahá'u'lláh accepted Badí''s request. Since it was not safe for Badí' to take the Tablet out of 'Akká, Bahá'u'lláh told him to go to Haifa and wait. There a believer handed Badí' the Tablet and he set out for Tehran at once. After four months, Badí' arrived in the city, intercepted the Shah to hand him the Tablet and was arrested, tortured and put to death. His martyrdom took place in June 1869.[17]

As Mírzá Mihdí was only four years older than Badí', might there have been a special relationship, albeit for a short time, between these two young Bahá'í luminaries, one named 'The Purest Branch', the other 'The Pride of Martyrs'?

* * *

It was from His small cell in the Most Great Prison that the supreme Manifestation of God addressed His historic epistles to the Turkish Prime Minister, Czar Alexander II, Pope Pius IX, Queen Victoria and the second Tablet to Napoleon III. The latter epistle was spirited out of the prison and delivered to Cesar Ketaphakou, son of the French Consul in 'Akká, who translated it into French and formally posted it to the sovereign. Cesar Ketaphakou eventually became a Bahá'í upon realizing that Napoleon III's downfall had taken place as Bahá'u'lláh had predicted in His Tablet.

It was through interactions such as this with Cesar Ketaphakou or with Dr Boutros, the local medic, or while going to the market, escorted by guards, to buy the daily victuals that the exiles began to socialize and build informal bridges with the broader community, eventually gaining their affection and respect, as well as winning a fine reputation that ultimately reached the Governor's ears. In *Vignettes from the Life of 'Abdu'l-Bahá* we find the following story:

> Early in the days of 'Abdu'l-Bahá's imprisonment in the barracks in 'Akká, news of His wisdom spread from a butcher's shop. He and a few of Bahá'u'lláh's companions had left the barracks to procure food and other necessary items from the markets. In the butcher's shop where the Master waited to be served, a Muslim and a Christian were apparently expounding

the merits of their respective faiths. The Christian was winning the discussion. Thereupon, 'Abdu'l-Bahá entered the conversation and with simplicity and eloquence proved the validity of Islam to the satisfaction of the Christian. The news of this incident spread and warmed the hearts of many people of 'Akká towards the Master; this was the beginning of His immense popularity among the inhabitants of that city.[18]

The prison guards, first-hand witnesses of the exiles' spiritual qualities and candour, gradually became more benign and sympathetic towards the group. It is known that Colonel Aḥmad-i-Jarráh, commander of the barracks, eventually became a Bahá'í, as did his brother, a government officer. 'Uthmán Effendi, the supplier of daily groceries to the group, became a Bahá'í and, as a result of a promise made by Bahá'u'lláh, prospered and became a very wealthy merchant.

History also remembers Shaykh Maḥmúd, a religious leader in 'Akká who had reportedly developed a deep antagonism to the Bahá'ís. In his mind, he could not tolerate the fact that the so-called 'God of the Persians', Bahá'u'lláh, had set foot in his city. One day Shaykh Maḥmúd, furious, grabbed 'Abdu'l-Bahá and rebuked Him, asking, 'Are you the son of God?'[19]

By that time, Shaykh Maḥmúd was so upset with Bahá'u'lláh's claim that He was a Manifestation of God that he decided to go the barracks with a gun hidden under his cloak to kill the Prophet of God. Because Shaykh Maḥmúd was a prominent citizen, the guards let him enter the prison. When Bahá'u'lláh was told that Shaykh Maḥmúd was waiting to see Him, He said to the guards, 'Tell him to cast away the weapon and then he may come in.'[20] Shaykh Maḥmúd was very perturbed by Bahá'u'lláh's clairvoyance and went home confused about the incident.

Later, he decided to go back to the barracks, this time without a weapon but determined to kill Bahá'u'lláh with his bare hands. When he asked the guards to meet Bahá'u'lláh, Shaykh Maḥmúd received this message from Him: 'Tell him to purify his heart first and then he may come in.'[21]

Baffled and disconcerted by this new token of divine wisdom he returned home and attempted to come to terms with his two attempts to murder Bahá'u'lláh. To add to his perplexity, one night he dreamt of an old shaykh and his father who had, when Shaykh Maḥmúd was a child, spoken to him regarding the eventual coming of the 'Promised One' to 'Akká. Later, he went to 'Abdu'l-Bahá and respectfully requested an interview with Bahá'u'lláh. The interview was granted.

Shaykh Maḥmúd entered Bahá'u'lláh's presence with the greatest humility, prostrating himself at His feet. He was now able to recognize Bahá'u'lláh's spiritual majesty and became a firm believer. Owing to his influence among the population and the government,

Shaykh Maḥmúd was able to facilitate the entry of pilgrims into the prison.

Shaykh 'Alíy-i-Mírí, the Muftí of 'Akká, was another person who met Bahá'u'lláh in the barracks. According to Ḥusayn-i-Áshchí's chronicle:

> He was a somewhat fanatical man. But later he changed as a result of his association with 'Abdu'l-Bahá. For he discovered that his own knowledge and learning was as a drop when compared with the ocean of 'Abdu'l-Bahá's innate knowledge. He therefore showed signs of humility and gradually became friendly.
>
> One day he conveyed to 'Abdu'l-Bahá his desire to meet Bahá'u'lláh as he had some questions and wished to be enlightened. But in those days Bahá'u'lláh did not grant interviews to people, mainly because He did not wish to act against the orders of the Government. However, because of 'Abdu'l-Bahá's pleading, Bahá'u'lláh gave permission and the Muftí of 'Akká attained His presence in the barracks. He was shown to his seat while 'Abdu'l-Bahá stood by the door. The kitchen in which I was working happened to be opposite the room of Bahá'u'lláh. I could see and hear Him. The Muftí asked some questions and then the Tongue of Grandeur began to speak. At one stage when the utterances of Bahá'u'lláh were still continuing, the Muftí was moved to say something. 'Abdu'l-Bahá gave him an emphatic and commanding signal with his hand

that he should not interrupt the words of Bahá'u'lláh. He complied but his pride was hurt.

When the interview was over he left, 'Abdu'l-Bahá accompanying him to the prison gate, but he was annoyed because of the incident, for he was well respected by the inhabitants of the town and as he walked in the bazaars people showed their respect to him and kissed his hands. At that stage he was not aware of the truth of the Cause and the greatness of its Author, therefore he was displeased with the way 'Abdu'l-Bahá had bidden him be silent. But it did not take very long before he realized that in the presence of 'Abdu'l-Bahá he was as utter nothingness. He used to visit the Master and partake of His knowledge and wisdom. He therefore changed his attitude. In the streets and bazaars, whenever he accompanied 'Abdu'l-Bahá he always walked a few steps behind Him and was never found to be walking in front. When Bahá'u'lláh was moved out of the barracks he used to come regularly to the outer apartment of the house – a room set aside for visitors – and sit at the feet of the Master. He diligently carried out every service that He referred to him.

As time went on the devotion of the Muftí of 'Akká towards Bahá'u'lláh and 'Abdu'l-Bahá increased. He became so attracted that once he intimated to 'Abdu'l-Bahá that every time he stood up to pray, the majestic figure of Bahá'u'lláh appeared before him. 'Abdu'l-Bahá always showered his favours upon the Muftí, as indeed on other prominent people in the land. It is true to say that a time came when the Government of 'Akká used to revolve around the person of 'Abdu'l-Bahá. Every one of the officials was longing to receive His blessings and favours. And because of His qualities and prestige the condition of the believers changed from abasement into honour.[22]

Nabíl-i-Qá'iní was another devoted pilgrim who arrived in 'Akká with his two sons. Having being identified and subsequently expelled from the prison-city, he settled in Nazareth, selling needles and exchanging them for eggs which he later sold to earn a meagre income. Eventually arrangements were made for him to come into the barracks and meet the Supreme Manifestation of God. 'When he entered there and lifted his eyes to the Blessed Beauty', 'Abdu'l-Bahá has related, 'he shook and trembled and fell unconscious to the floor. Bahá'u'lláh spoke words of loving-kindness to him and he rose again. He spent some days hidden in the barracks, after which he returned to Nazareth.'[23]

In different ways, taking every chance and facing serious risks, these first Bahá'í pilgrims, some with greater success than others, tried to circumvent the restrictions as they sought their Beloved's presence. One even dressed as a local Arab and hired a camel and was thus able to set foot inside the prison-city.

Equally interesting is the elderly Ustád Ismá'íl from Ká<u>sh</u>án, who, according to the testimony of Shoghi Effendi, the Guardian of the Bahá'í Faith,

> ... arriving from Mosul, posted himself on the far side of the moat, and, gazing for hours, in rapt adoration, at the window of his Beloved, failed in the end, owing to the feebleness of his sight, to discern His face, and had to turn back to the cave which served as his dwelling-place on Mt. Carmel – an episode that moved to tears the Holy Family who had been anxiously watching from afar the frustration of his hopes.[24]

Of Ustád Ismá'íl, the one-time prosperous government constructor who had become the deprived pilgrim, for whom the word 'privilege' was more about nearness to Bahá'u'lláh than anything else, 'Abdu'l-Bahá wrote:

> He was like a bird with broken wings but he had the song and it kept him going onward to his one true Love. By stealth, he approached the Fortress and went in, but he was exhausted, spent. He remained for some days, and came into the presence of Bahá'u'lláh, after which he was directed to look for a lodging in Haifa. He got himself to Haifa, but he found no haven there, no nest or hole, no water, no grain of corn. Finally he made his home in a cave outside the town. He acquired a little tray and on this he set out rings of earthenware,

and some thimbles, pins and other trinkets. Every day, from morning till noon, he peddled these, wandering about. Some days his earnings would amount to twenty paras, some days thirty; and forty on his best days. Then he would go home to the cave and content himself with a piece of bread. He was always voicing his thanks, always saying, 'Praise be to God that I have attained such favour and grace; that I have been separated from friend and stranger alike, and have taken refuge in this cave. Now I am of those who gave their all, to buy the Divine Joseph in the market place. What bounty could be any greater than this!'[25]

Another of these pilgrims was Áqá 'Alíy-i-Qazvíní, whose pilgrimage was described by 'Abdu'l-Bahá:

The day came when he set out for the Most Great Prison, and arrived with his family at the 'Akká fortress. He had been afflicted with many a hardship on his journey, but his longing to see Bahá'u'lláh was such that he found the calamities easy to endure; and so he measured off the miles, looking for a home in God's sheltering grace.

At first he had means; life was comfortable and pleasant. Later on, however, he was destitute and subjected to terrible ordeals. Most of the time his food was bread, nothing else; instead of tea, he drank from a running brook. Still, he remained happy and content.

His great joy was to enter the presence of Bahá'u'lláh; reunion with his Beloved was bounty enough; his food was to look upon the beauty of the Manifestation; his wine, to be with Bahá'u'lláh. He was always smiling, always silent; but at the same time, his heart shouted, leapt and danced.[26]

Mírzá Asadu'lláh Káshání described his own epic journey from Iraq to 'Akká:

As soon as we knew that the Beloved Ones were at 'Akká, I started off with a Persian Bahá'í, who, having escaped from Dahají, had joined the band of exiles at Mosul. We determined to make our way to 'Akká. We walked six or seven hours a day, and coming to Aleppo we rested; thence we walked to Damascus.

Oh, how happy we were as we walked, each step bringing us nearer to the presence of Jamál-i-Mubárak [literally, Blessed Beauty, i.e. Bahá'u'lláh] and Sarkár-i-Áqá [literally, the Master, i.e. 'Abdu'l-Bahá].

Sometimes we sheltered for a night in the tent of a Bedouin, who welcomed us with unfailing kind hospitality; again we slept under the stars, with stones for our pillows, always with songs of joy in our hearts, because of our destination.

That preoccupation of the Spirit, as in our journey from Baghdad to Mosul, upheld us, and made all hardships so unimportant that we forgot them.

Entrance into the citadel, the Most Great Prison

The door on the left leads to Bahá'u'lláh's cell

Bahá'u'lláh's cell in the citadel

Bahá'u'lláh's cell, refurbished in 2004

The two windows on the far right on the top floor of the citadel are in the cell occupied by Bahá'u'lláh

The window in Bahá'u'lláh's cell through which He would extend His hand to greet the pilgrims unable to enter the citadel

View from the refurbished window today

Abu'l-Ḥasan-i-Ardikání (Ḥájí Amín), the first pilgrim to meet Bahá'u'lláh within 'Akká's walls

Badí', who, dressed as a water-carrier bearing the tools of his trade, was introduced into the barracks and attained Bahá'u'lláh's presence

The roof of the prison where Mírzá Mihdí walked

*Photo map of northern section, city of 'Akká (1975)
Cell of Bahá'u'lláh (1), western section where Holy Family was held (2), approximate site of skylight over eastern section (3), sections of barracks-prison (4), citadel (5), barrack-square, formerly a khán (6), former governorate building (7) and its courtroom (8), Mosque of al-Jazzár (9), madrisih, religious school of the mosque (10), Sharí'ah Court of the 'Akká district (11), White Súq of 'Umar and Sulaymán (12), inner moat, northern defences (13), public bath of al-Jazzár, now the 'Akká Municipal Museum (14).*

The skylight, refurbished, through which Mírzá Mihdí fell onto a wooden crate below

During the restoration of the prison it was decided to leave untouched the floor where Mírzá Mihdí fell. The stairs to the roof are in the background.

The Nabí Ṣáliḥ cemetery on the outskirts of 'Akká where Mírzá Mihdí was first buried. His headstone is on the right.

The Nabí Ṣáliḥ cemetery in 2017. Note the space where the grave of Mírzá Mihdí originally stood

The original headstone over Mírzá Mihdí's grave at the Nabí Ṣáliḥ cemetery

The House of 'Abbúd, one of the houses in which Bahá'u'lláh and His family lived after they left the citadel. Navváb passed away in this house

At length we came to Damascus, where, finding a friend from my native village, also a coppersmith, I tarried with him for ten days.

Then we started off again over the beautiful snowy Lebanon mountains, where the hospitable Bedouins were as ever our friends, and so we came to Beirut, where we rested for a week.

And now the last part of our pilgrimage from Beirut to 'Akká. I disguised myself as a dervish. Very seldom did I think it wise to ask to be directed, therefore we often wandered out of our way.

Our exaltation grew. Oh, the loveliness of the land through which we walked, the fragrance of the orange groves, the beauty of the many coloured flowers which carpeted the plains!

We stayed one night in the town of Sidon, surrounded with its luxuriant fruit trees, the scent of which is so delicious; then a night at Tyre. As we walked the 'Ladder of Tyre' we saw 'Akká in the distance, shining in the sun, and there, in that place were our Beloved Ones.

Great was the caution needed. We arrived separately.

My disguise allowed me to enter the city unquestioned. I wandered about in perplexity, for I did not dare to ask for information as to the abode of the Holy Ones. Fatigue was beginning to overwhelm me.

At length I went to the mosque, where I found a Shaykh who lived near by. I discovered that he was a Bahá'í; 'Alláh'u'Abhá.' When he knew of my journey and of my aim, he said: 'Stay here with me, the Master will come when it is evening time.'

I waited, breathless with anticipation.

Then from the mosque came our beloved Master!

He was young then and very beautiful.

'Aḥvál-i-S̲h̲umá? Marḥabá! Marḥabá! K̲h̲aylí K̲h̲ush ámadíd.' ('How are you? Welcome! Welcome! Your coming gives me most great pleasure and delight.')

His loving-kindness restored my soul. I was ready to sacrifice my life to *once* hear His 'Marḥabá!'

'How tired you must be after that long, long, toilsome journey. I will send one of the friends to you in the morning.'

So I rested in ecstatic peace, having achieved the desire of my heart.

In the morning Áqá Faraj came and took me to the K̲h̲án (inn) where four or five friends were staying. This was, of course, very secretly and cautiously arranged because of the threatened grave danger, at this time never absent from any suspected of being Bahá'ís. I rested quietly at the K̲h̲án, recovering from the physical fatigues of the journey.

After fifteen days, I was commanded to fetch my mother and my younger brother from Aleppo, where they were awaiting directions, having journeyed from Mosul, sometimes by steamer, and sometimes riding on mules.

How glad I was that my dear ones were to come into the presence of Jamál-i-Mubárak and the Master, Sarkár-i-Áqá! I joyfully departed on my errand, walking to Haifa, thence by boat to Alexandretta, thence to Aleppo. Returning with my family the same way, we arrived at Haifa. There we heard that my mother would be received into the holy household, to her extreme delight. My brother and I, however, were to remain at Haifa, not being suffered to go inside the town of 'Akká.

We therefore remained at Haifa, working at our trade of coppersmith. We opened a little shop. I went round to the houses, selling things that we had made.

My brother and I prospered at our work.

We used frequently to walk over by way of the sea, wading through the brook Kishon to 'Akká.

We would stand in a certain place, without the wall of the prison, and watch a particular window; sometimes we had the joy of seeing the hand of Bahá'u'lláh waving a greeting to us. We would then walk back to Haifa, delighted to have had our reward.[27]

Like Mírzá Asadu'lláh Káshání, Ustád Ismá'íl, Nabíl-i-A'zam, Nabíl-i-Qá'iní, Badí', Abu'l-Ḥasan-i-Ardikání and Áqá 'Alíy-i-Qazvíní, many others had to wait for the severity of the imprisonment to lessen before they were able to surreptitiously enter the barracks, some wandering in the area for long periods as they waited.

Such hardships brought great sorrow to the Holy Family, which watched the pilgrims with anxiety from the prison windows.

The story of another Persian pilgrim, 'Abdu'r-Raḥím, narrated by Adib Taherzadeh, recalls the tension arising from the strict confinement of Bahá'u'lláh and His party and the perseverance of the Bahá'ís to reach their Beloved by any means:

> For six months 'Abdu'r-Raḥím travelled on foot until he reached the abode of his Beloved – the prison city of 'Akká. He arrived in the early days of Bahá'u'lláh's incarceration in the barracks when no visitor suspected of being a Bahá'í was permitted even to approach the vicinity of the prison. His arrival coincided with the period when Nabíl-i-A'ẓam was attempting in vain to get a glimpse of his Lord. Nabíl poured out his heart to 'Abdu'r-Raḥím and lamented over his own inability to achieve his purpose. But 'Abdu'r-Raḥím, undismayed, proceeded to attempt to circumambulate the prison.
>
> Before undertaking such a holy mission, he decided that he must wash his clothes, which were unclean, as they had been worn throughout the journey. He washed them in the sea and waited until they were dry. When he put them on, however, he looked very odd and shabby as the clothes had shrunk and were torn.
>
> With the utmost devotion and a heart overflowing

with the love of Bahá'u'lláh, 'Abdu'r-Raḥím approached the prison and began to circumambulate it. Then to his surprise he noticed that a hand from a window of the prison was beckoning him to come inside. He knew it was the hand of Bahá'u'lláh summoning him to His presence. He rushed to the gate of the prison which was guarded by soldiers. But the soldiers seemed to him to be motionless and without life; they appeared not to see him. They did not even move an eyelid as he went through the gate.

Soon 'Abdu'r-Raḥím found himself in the presence of His Lord, overwhelmed by emotion and carried away into the world of the Spirit, communing with the One who was the object of his adoration and love. Bahá'u'lláh told him that through the hands of power and might He had temporarily blinded the eyes of the guards so that he might attain His presence as a bounty on His part.

It is not clear how many days 'Abdu'r-Raḥím remained in the prison. However, Bahá'u'lláh revealed a Tablet for him while he was there. In that Tablet He confirms that He had closed the eyes of the guards so that 'Abdu'r-Raḥím could enter His presence and witness the glory of His countenance. He calls him by the new name Raḥím (Compassionate), showers His blessings upon him, and urges him to recount the experience of his pilgrimage to the friends on his return home.[28]

Such an abyss of anguish and distress, caused by the Sultan of Turkey separating the Bahá'ís from their Beloved, is sensed in the following words revealing Bahá'u'lláh's pain: 'Later We entered this Prison, wherein the hands of Our loved ones were torn from the hem of Our robe. In such a manner hath he dealt with Us!'[29]

Mírzá Mihdí's sacrifice would be the instrument by which the prison doors would open so that Bahá'ís could finally enter the holy presence of the Abhá Beauty.

9

The Treasure of God in the Holy Land

Rising above the 'Akká terrain, the massive quadrangular prison tower where the Holy Family was imprisoned will be remembered by history as an imposing memorial to captivity and tyranny. Built as an impressively tall structure, its walls contained many windows on every side, like eyes watching the sea on the horizon, the adjacent military installations and the neighbouring city streets.

Life in 'Akká began before the sun greeted the earth with its light. The call to prayer, with its summoning strains, awakened the population both spiritually and physically. The chatter of busy women could be heard as they hung their washing over their high-topped balconies. The smell of traditional homemade recipes handed down from mother to daughter over generations could be discerned within even the most desolate of alleyways. If there was anything beautiful in 'Akká it was its sunrise, so brilliant and promising. It trumpeted not only the beginning of the new day but the thrust that life goes on regardless of any spatial or temporal limitation or difficulty.

There was also something strange and ghostly about the nights in 'Akká. Stars replaced people in a matter of hours, taking away the hustle and bustle from the streets and leaving the secluded city with an air of a spiritual vacuum. The ambitions and aspirations of the commoner were laid to rest until the next day. The waves of the sea, the absolute human silence and the hooting of the owls then began to haunt the prisoners, reminding them of the spell surrounding this magical and millenary place, 'one of the oldest continuously-inhabited cities in the world, as well as one of the most fought-over'.[1] This was, after all, a legendary city, whose streets were trodden by personages such as Alexander the Great, Julius Caesar, St Paul, Marco Polo and Maimonides, not to mention Napoleon, who stood so aggressively and yet powerlessly at its walls. The very barracks were built on the ruins of a Crusader citadel, adding mystery to this already cryptic site. This was the city whose nightly darkness could be as lugubrious as its spiritual obscurity. Although it was the land of promise, it was also the place of negation. Soon, momentous events were to unfold, one after the other.

The local inhabitants, oblivious of the spiritual supremacy of the newly-arrived Personage living in that solitary tower, carried out their daily domestic duties as usual. 'Akká, with its high stoned walls, guarded this most precious Prophet, and yet its people were unaware that He was the One promised by the holy books of the past. On one hand, the walls of this much-prophesied prison city were calling out that the Promised One was amongst them; on the other, the locals, wrapt in their spiritual slumber, were unable to perceive that call which for centuries they had been longing to hear.

But for those living within the barracks, life that very first morning after the arrival of the exiles was different: They had woken up locked in a real prison in small rooms. Nonetheless, being with God's Supreme Manifestation was for the exiles both a blessing and a confirmation. It was a blessing because they felt that divine guidance was with them, day by day, rich and ceaselessly, embracing their own lives. It was also a confirmation since the real Sun was with them, radiating life and grace while its celestial counterpart was imparting warm and light from above.

Whilst in the citadel, Mírzá Mihdí often used to attain the presence of Bahá'u'lláh in the afternoon, remaining until he completed his tasks. Afterwards, it was his custom to go up to the roof and spend the remaining time in prayer and meditation. On the roof one could breathe better quality air away from the pestilence and dampness of the lower reaches of the prison, and obtain a good view as well as listen to the sound of the waves washing the bay – a moment of spiritual peace and calm.

One hot afternoon Mírzá Mihdí was occupied with his devotions on the roof and afterwards went, as always, to Bahá'u'lláh's chamber to fulfil his usual secretarial duties. Because he did not feel well, it was suggested that he return to the roof. Several other Bahá'í prisoners were also unwell. It seems that Bahá'u'lláh told Mírzá Mihdí, 'I will not need you tonight.'[2]

Mírzá Mihdí went up the narrow stairs and began his devotions, walking to and fro across the roof. Absorbed in his meditations and invocations, raising and lowering his head, he knew the number of steps that should be taken to avoid falling through the unguarded skylight that provided light and ventilation to the floor ten metres below.

It was nearing nightfall and the sky was darkening, moonless, as the local people returned to their homes. Sunset on that day was at 7:12 p.m. The daily bustle abated and the lights of households were gradually lit. For the inhabitants of the city, who were unaware of the spiritual drama unfolding in their neighbouring prison, the tragic event that took place that evening meant nothing. And who could imagine that anything greater than the afflictions already suffered by the exiles would occur? The desolation of the prison, its miseries and loathsome environment, the exiles deprived of family ties and alienated from friends, the indifference of the local population, the innumerable hardships, the manifest injustice and the complete isolation made it difficult for the exiles to think of anything more appalling.

But the decree of Providence should never be second-guessed. 'It is for God to test His servants, and not for His servants to judge Him in accordance with their deficient standards,' the Báb said.³ From time immemorial we have known that God's ways should not be questioned. As the Blessed Beauty wrote:

> I swear by My life! Nothing save that which profiteth them can befall My loved ones. To this testifieth the Pen of God, the Most Powerful, the All-Glorious, the Best Beloved.⁴

At twilight, as darkness began to fall over the horizon of the Mediterranean, Mírzá Mihdí was still observing his vigil on the prison roof. He was reciting the poignant passages of the Ode of the Dove, a mystical treatise of 127 verses, written when Bahá'u'lláh had retired to the mountains of Sulaymáníyyih, in which He speaks of His grief and suffering:

> Noah's flood is but the measure of the tears I have shed, and Abraham's fire an ebullition of My soul. Jacob's grief is but a reflection of My sorrows, and Job's afflictions a fraction of my calamity.⁵

Mírzá Mihdí was captivated by the tone of deep

distress in the words of his father. Without realizing it, being in a state of prayer, he stumbled, lost his balance and fell through the open skylight onto a wooden crate standing on the floor beneath. He fell into the area used as a living room, near the kitchen. No one was there at the time.

The sound of the impact and the groans of the Purest Branch immediately drew the attention of those who were nearby. They rushed to see what had happened. All were shocked and frightened by the scene; they barely believed what they saw. Why would God decree that such tragedy be added to their burdens? What was the wisdom hidden in this new misfortune?

We can picture in our minds what they saw. Mírzá Mihdí was bleeding profusely from his mouth. The wooden crate had shattered and splinters were embedded in his ribs and thigh to the extent that it was impossible to remove his clothes, which later had to be torn from him.

Navváb (Ásíyih Khánum), Mírzá Mihdí's mother, 'frail and weeping', also went to her son's side as he lay below the open skylight. Seeing her son soaked in blood, she was plunged into an agonizing anguish and fainted away.[6] Mírzá Mihdí took her in his arms to consol her.

Bahá'u'lláh Himself came to Mírzá Mihdí. Bahíyyih Khánum relates:

The Blessed Perfection, hearing the commotion, opened the door of his room and looked out. When he saw his son he turned back and re-entered his room, saying: 'Mahdy [Mihdí] has gone!'[7]

Ḥusayn-i-Áshchí, the cook to the Holy Family and an eyewitness, described those tragic moments:

> The terrific loud sound of the impact made us all run to the scene of the tragedy where we beheld in astonishment what had happened as decreed by God, and were so shocked as to beat upon our heads. Then the Ancient Beauty came out of His room and asked what he had done which caused his fall. The Purest Branch said that he knew the whereabouts of the skylight and in the past had been careful not to come near it, but this time it was his fate to forget about it.[8]

Many years later Effie Baker, having been on pilgrimage, confirmed this account, writing to the Australian Bahá'ís that

> Baha'u'llah and his [Mírzá Mihdí's] mother heard the noise and Baha'u'llah said 'That's my Mahdi, he has been sacrificed.' They went out and he was lying on the floor with his bones broken. They carried him to a room and put him on a couch.[9]

The 'blood-stained shirt worn by Bahá'u'lláh as He attended the dying Purest Branch' was given many years later to the National Spiritual Assembly of the Bahá'ís of Iraq by Shoghi Effendi.[10]

With great care, Mírzá Mihdí, still conscious, was taken to his room.[11] Everyone, desperate, gathered around his bed.

An Italian doctor was called but Mírzá Mihdí's injuries were so serious that he could not do much for him, nor was there a hospital in 'Akká. In the midst of his overwhelming pain, Mírzá Mihdí's nobility was clear to all, as he apologized to those who came to his bedside.

'In spite of much pain and agony,' a witness recounted, 'and being weak, he warmly greeted those who came to his bedside, showered an abundance of love and favours upon them and apologized to everyone, saying he was ashamed that while they were all sitting, he had to lie down in their presence.'[12]

So distressed was 'Abdu'l-Bahá that with His heart in His hand and His eyes filled with tears He entered the presence of Bahá'u'lláh, kneeled at His feet and implored Him to heal His young brother.

'O my Greatest Branch, leave him in the hands of his God' was Bahá'u'lláh's response.[13]

The historian Nabíl tells us that the grief-stricken Navváb also went to the Blessed Perfection, kneeled down and implored Him:

'My Lord, I entreat Thee to accept from me this ransom.' The Blessed Beauty conferred His bountiful favours upon her and advised her to be patient. Ásíyih Khánum responded: 'Whatever is Thy good-pleasure that indeed is my heart's desire and my best beloved . . .'[14]

The Blessed Perfection went to Mírzá Mihdí's room and for a long time they were alone. We do not know what they discussed – father and son took the content of their conversation to the next world of God. This was Mírzá Mihdí's last private meeting on earth with the Manifestation of God, both enclosed in the solitude of the young man's cell with the desperate believers congregating outside, crying and praying. If, owing to Mírzá Mihdí's extreme injuries and agony, the encounter was wordless, what might Bahá'u'lláh with His divine powers have offered His son to ease his agony and his inevitable death? Did Bahá'u'lláh show him the wonders and marvels of the worlds of God? Was it the vision of the believers living in freedom? Was it perhaps a preview of the unified humankind to which Mírzá Mihdí's life was dedicated? If words were spoken, were they words of consolation such that any father in similar circumstances would say to his child? We do know that the Supreme Manifestation of God had the power to bring people back to life (as we have seen in the story of Mírzá Ja'far in chapter 7), and we also know when he was on his deathbed yet still conscious, Mírzá Mihdí was asked by Bahá'u'lláh if he wanted Him to save his life.

'What do you desire?' the Blessed Beauty asked him. 'Do you wish to live, or do you prefer to die? Tell me what you most wish for.'

With great magnanimity the Purest Branch replied, 'I don't care to live. I have but one wish. I want the believers to be admitted to see their Lord. If you will promise me this, it is all I ask.'

Bahá'u'lláh accepted His son's noble request and told him that it would be so.[15]

By respecting Mírzá Mihdí's desire and therefore denying Himself the opportunity to save His son, Bahá'u'lláh must have been heartbroken. Yet the Manifestations of God see realities that ordinary beings cannot even imagine: 'Were We to recount the mysteries of thine ascension,' Bahá'u'lláh later wrote, 'they that are asleep would waken, and all beings would be set ablaze with the fire of the remembrance of My Name, the Mighty, the Loving.'[16]

Following what must have been a horrible night for him and the Holy Family, the next day Mírzá Mihdí asked to meet the believers, whom he received with the utmost love and kindness. However, so serious were his injuries that death took him away that evening. The agony of the Purest Branch lasted for 22 hours. On Thursday, 23 June 1870, when he was 22 years old,

Mírzá Mihdí passed away, ascending to the Supreme Concourse so suddenly and tragically.

It is impossible to describe the depth of the consternation that seized all at that moment of grief. Bahá'u'lláh, his dear father and Lord, greatly affected by the sudden and untimely loss, was heard lamenting, 'O Mihdí! O Mihdí!'[17]

For Navváb, this was the fifth time she had lost a son during her lifetime, three in Iran, one in Baghdad and now Mírzá Mihdí in the military barracks. Undoubtedly this was an affliction and a test too great to bear for a mother and a believer. Heartbroken and inconsolable in her grief, she gained strength only when her husband told her that giving their son to the Cause of God so that the believers could visit their Lord was in itself a meritorious deed in the eyes of God. According to Bahíyyih Khánum:

> The death of this youngest and favourite child – of a very gentle and sweet disposition – nearly broke his mother's heart. We feared for her reason. When the Blessed Perfection was told of the condition of his wife, he went to her and said: 'Your son has been taken by God that His people might be freed. His life was the ransom, and you should rejoice that you had a son so dear to give to the cause of God.' When our mother heard these words she seemed to rally, – knelt, and kissed the Blessed Perfection's hands, and thanked

him for what he had said. After that she did not shed a tear.[18]

'Abdu'l-Bahá, the Master, who had been Mírzá Mihdí's close companion in exile, was also heartsick amid the universal outpouring of tears and grief, as was Bahíyyih Khánum, Mírzá Mihdí's beloved older sister. A sea of sadness engulfed everyone.

Bahíyyih Khánum said of those tragic moments:

> So, after much patient suffering, my brother's gentle spirit took its flight. As we could not leave the barracks, we could not bury our dead; nor had we the consolation of feeling that we could provide for him through others the grateful final tribute of a proper and fitting burial, as we had no means wherewith even to purchase a coffin. After some consideration and consultation among ourselves, finding that we had nothing to dispose of, and at a loss how to proceed, we told our Lord of the sad situation. He replied that there was a rug in his room which we could sell. At first we demurred, for in taking his rug we took the only comfort he had; but he insisted and we sold it. A coffin was then procured, and the remains of my deceased brother placed in it. It was carried out by our jailors, and we did not even know whither it was taken.[19]

An eyewitness recalled the funeral preparations:

> ... Shaykh Maḥmúd begged the Master to allow him to have the honour of washing the body and not to let anyone from the city of 'Akká perform this service. The Master gave permission. A tent was pitched in the middle of the barracks. We placed his blessed body upon a table in the middle of the tent and Shaykh Maḥmúd began the task of washing it. The loved ones of God were wailing and lamenting with tearful eyes and, like unto moths, were circling around that candle which the hands of God had lighted. I brought water in and was involved in washing the body. The Master was pacing up and down outside the tent. His face betrayed signs of deep sorrow ...
>
> The body after being washed and shrouded was placed inside a new casket. At this moment the cry of weeping and mourning and sore lamentation rose up to the heavens. The casket was carried high on the shoulders of men out of the barracks with utmost serenity and majesty.[20]

Baharieh Rouhani Ma'ani tells us that

> The body of the Purest Branch was washed in the barracks before the eyes of Bahá'u'lláh. The traditional restrictions on women probably compelled Ásíyih Khánum to remain in the upper floor of the barracks,

where the family lived, and mourn the loss of her beloved son away from where his body was being washed.[21]

The believers were not allowed to accompany the coffin to its resting place and it was reported that the location of the burial was unknown to them for two years.[22] It has been stated that the notables of ʿAkká accompanied the funeral procession.[23] The believers, however, could only see a small procession carrying their fellow exile, the 'pious and holy youth',[24] as Mírzá Mihdí was described by Shoghi Effendi, taken through the land gate, through which he had never before passed. His body was interred in the Nabí Ṣáliḥ (Prophet Ṣáliḥ) cemetery outside the fortress.

As the guards returned to the prison, a strong earth tremor occurred across a large radius. Felt as far away as Nazareth, the tremor lasted three minutes, frightening local inhabitants. Baháʾuʾlláh confirms this in a tribute to His martyred son:

> When thou wast laid to rest in the earth, the earth itself trembled in its longing to meet thee. Thus hath it been decreed, and yet the people perceive not . . .[25]

Soon after Mírzá Mihdí's sacrifice conditions in the prison were relaxed. In November 1870, in the middle of autumn, little more than four months after the tragedy, his wish was fulfilled, giving God's answer to his yearning request. It was just as Bahá'u'lláh had prophesied in these words addressed to His martyred son: 'Thou art, verily, the trust of God and His treasure in this land. Erelong will God reveal through thee that which He hath desired.'[26]

Mírzá Mihdí had sacrificed his life for the happiness of the Bahá'ís and so that believers would have access to the presence of Bahá'u'lláh. A tense international situation with Russia caused the Turkish government to reorganize its army, making it necessary to once again use the 'Akká barracks as an army facility. Thus just a few weeks after Mírzá Mihdí's martyrdom the barracks were flooded by military personnel and their equipment. According to David Ruhe:

> Bahá'u'lláh protested at the crowding and problems produced by the soldiers; hence, early in November 1870, the governor allowed the Great Prisoner and His followers to leave the barracks to live in the city under house confinement and surveillance.[27]

Bahíyyih Khánum recalls that

> Some time after the death of his son, the Blessed Perfection (who, as I have said, usually never attended to affairs, these being all left to my brother) expressed a wish to have an interview with the Governor.

MÍRZÁ MIHDÍ

Meanwhile my brother's dying prayer, that the believers might be permitted to visit their Lord, having been overheard by a soldier who was present at the time and by him repeated to the officer in charge, had come to the ears of the Governor. Very possibly it had touched him and now influenced him to accede to the Blessed Perfection's request for an interview; at all events the request was granted, and the Blessed Perfection met the Governor in council with his officers. He then addressed them on the subject of his separation from his followers and of their great sorrow and distress occasioned by it, reminding them of his deceased son's dying petition, and speaking with such eloquence and power that the Governor was moved to grant his appeal.

We were, in consequence, removed from the barracks and given a comfortable house with three rooms and a court. Our people, and also our family, were permitted to go at large in the city, and whoever wished could visit us; but my father was required to remain within the house.[28]

Whatever the details, the prison doors were opened after the passing of the Purest Branch and the pilgrims were given more access to the Manifestation of God. All the exiles eventually left the prison barracks with the loving memory of the four who did not: Muḥammad-Ismá'il, Muḥammad-Báqír, Abu'l-Qásim and Mírzá Mihdí.

With this glorious liberation, the Bahá'ís and pilgrims were finally able to reach the presence of the Manifestation of God as He proclaimed:

Verily I say, this is the Day in which mankind can behold the Face, and hear the Voice, of the Promised One.[29]

10

The Great Redemptive Sacrifice of the Purest Branch

On the very day of Mírzá Mihdí's passing Bahá'u'lláh revealed a Tablet to the Bahá'ís of Qazvin which expresses His grief and testifies to the exalted position of that 'Branch of God',[1] the 'Trust of God', who had been 'created of the light of Bahá', and of 'His treasure' in the Holy Land:[2]

> At this very moment My son is being washed before My face, after Our having sacrificed him in the Most Great Prison. Thereat have the dwellers of the Abhá Tabernacle wept with a great weeping, and such as have suffered imprisonment with this Youth in the path of God, the Lord of the promised Day, lamented. Under such conditions My Pen hath not been prevented from remembering its Lord, the Lord of all nations. It summoneth the people unto God, the Almighty, the All-Bountiful. This is the day whereon he that was created by the light of Bahá has suffered martyrdom, at a time when he lay imprisoned at the hands of his enemies . . .

THE GREAT REDEMPTIVE SACRIFICE OF THE PUREST BRANCH

> Upon thee, O Branch of God! be the remembrance of God and His praise, and the praise of all that dwell in the Realm of Immortality, and of all the denizens of the Kingdom of Names. Happy art thou in that thou hast been faithful to the Covenant of God and His Testament, until Thou didst sacrifice thyself before the face of thy Lord, the Almighty, the Unconstrained. Thou, in truth, hast been wronged, and to this testifieth the Beauty of Him, the Self-Subsisting. Thou didst, in the first days of thy life, bear that which hath caused all things to groan, and made every pillar to tremble. Happy is the one that remembereth thee, and draweth nigh, through thee, unto God, the Creator of the Morn.[3]

Shoghi Effendi commented on the powerful meanings permeating Mírzá Mihdí's sacrifice, a sacrifice which unleashed the spiritual energies required for the unification of all humanity:

> In a highly significant prayer, revealed by Bahá'u'lláh in memory of His son – a prayer that exalts his death to the rank of those great acts of atonement associated with Abraham's intended sacrifice of His son, with the crucifixion of Jesus Christ and the martyrdom of the Imám Ḥusayn – we read the following: 'I have, O my Lord, offered up that which Thou hast given Me, that Thy servants may be quickened, and all that dwell on earth be united.'[4]

MÍRZÁ MIHDÍ

The historian Adib Taherzadeh in volume 3 of his series *The Revelation of Bahá'u'lláh* wrote about the deep significance of Mírzá Mihdí's martyrdom in the chain of the progressive revelation of God's Faith:

> In another instance, Shoghi Effendi states that in the Bábí Dispensation, it was the Báb himself who sacrificed His life for the redemption and purification of mankind. In the Dispensation of Bahá'u'lláh, it was the Purest Branch who gave his life releasing thereby all the forces necessary for bringing about the unity of mankind.[5]

Finally, it is appropriate to remember the lifelong suffering of this unique being in the words of Bahá'u'lláh as He communed with His Creator:

> Lauded be Thy name, O Lord my God! Thou seest me in this day shut up in my prison, and fallen into the hands of Thine adversaries, and beholdest my son (The Purest Branch) lying on the dust before Thy face. He is Thy servant, O my Lord, whom Thou hast caused to be related to Him Who is the Manifestation of Thyself and the Day-Spring of Thy Cause.
>
> At his birth he was afflicted through his separation from Thee, according to what had been ordained for him through Thine irrevocable decree. And when he had quaffed the cup of reunion with Thee, he was

cast into prison for having believed in Thee and in Thy signs. He continued to serve Thy Beauty until he entered into this Most Great Prison. Thereupon I offered him up, O my God, as a sacrifice in Thy path. Thou well knowest what they who love Thee have endured through this trial that hath caused the kindreds of the earth to wail, and beyond them the Concourse on high to lament.[6]

Glorified art Thou, O Lord, my God! Thou seest me in the hands of Mine enemies, and My son bloodstained before Thy face, O Thou in Whose hands is the kingdom of all names. I have, O my Lord, offered up that which Thou hast given Me, that Thy servants may be quickened and all that dwell on earth be united.[7]

Blessed art thou, and blessed he that turneth unto thee, and visiteth thy grave, and draweth nigh, through thee, unto God, the Lord of all that was and shall be . . . I testify that thou didst return in meekness unto thine abode. Great is thy blessedness and the blessedness of them that hold fast unto the hem of thy outspread robe . . .[8]

In 1970 the Universal House of Justice called upon the entire Baháʼí world to unite in prayer to commemorate the centenary of Mírzá Mihdí's martyrdom, whose sacrifice was accepted by Baháʼu'lláh as a 'ransom' for 'the regeneration of the world and the unification of its peoples'.⁹ The report of the dignified and solemn commemoration at the Bahá'í World Centre reads:

> On the morning of June 23, 1970, the hundredth anniversary of the tragic death of Mírzá Mihdí, the Purest Branch, the Hand of the Cause Paul Haney, and members of the Universal House of Justice, gathered at the barracks in the prison city of 'Akká to offer prayers in the cell which Bahá'u'lláh had occupied for two years, two months and five days following His arrival in 'Akká in 1868. The scene of the martyrdom was also visited and a prayer chanted there.
>
> Immediately afterwards the party proceeded to Bahjí where they joined others serving at the World Centre and approximately eighty pilgrims who came from many countries.
>
> All walked around the Ḥarám-i-Aqdas and down the path to the Shrine of Bahá'u'lláh where the Tablet of Visitation was recited.
>
> Towards sunset the friends assembled on Mt. Carmel at the twin monuments of the Purest Branch and his saintly mother, Navváb, to conclude the programme commemorating the centenary of the martyrdom. Prayers and verses appropriate to the occasion were read and chanted.
>
> Thus at the spiritual heart of the Bahá'í world was honoured the memory of a blessed youth whose life

was offered up for the quickening of the spirits of the servants of Bahá'u'lláh and hastening of the unity and promised redemption of mankind.[10]

11

Life without Mírzá Mihdí

The cemetery where Mírzá Mihdí was first laid to rest lies just outside the eastern city wall of 'Akká, 600 metres away from the barracks, near the land gate. His grave was adjacent to the shrine of a holy man, Nabí Ṣáliḥ, regarded as the patron saint of the city. Mírzá Mihdí's interment was an unusual one: no friends, no family and therefore no tears or flowers. On that summer day the soldiers took the plain brown coffin to a spot close to the main shrine of the Prophet Ṣáliḥ in the cemetery. It seems that the episode attracted some public attention because it is reported that the city notables accompanied the funeral procession, and therefore they may well have held some kind of religious service at the graveside.

The grave was probably later visited by the pilgrims banned from the Most Great Prison yet able to say prayers at the rudimentary grave of the Purest Branch, thus observing Bahá'u'lláh's exhortation, '. . . blessed he that turneth unto thee, and visiteth thy grave . . .'[1] They must have approached the solitary tomb lying at the shrine wall with sadness but also with reverence. This was a sanctified spot, the first such in the Holy

LIFE WITHOUT MÍRZÁ MIHDÍ

Land. With time, the cemetery of Nabí Ṣáliḥ was populated with the remains of another 13 believers who passed away at the Most Great Prison over a period of 12 years, keeping earthly company with the Purest Branch buried nearby.

Mírzá Mihdí's memory was always fresh in the minds of the believers in the years following his death and burial, and he continued to be held in much affection. One believer whose memory of the Purest Branch was strong was Nabíl-i-Qá'iní, a Bahá'í resident in Nazareth. He had met Bahá'u'lláh in the barracks years before (see chapter 8) and had experienced in Nazareth, 32 km away, the strong earthquake that occurred at the very time that Mírzá Mihdí was buried (see chapter 9). The friends used to refer to him with reverence as 'Mihdí Effendi' or 'His Holiness the Branch'.

One day Nabíl-i-Qá'iní was walking in the bazaar and met a number of believers as well as the local gravedigger. He persuaded them to accompany him to the Nabí Ṣáliḥ cemetery. There he told them, 'I have a request to make of you: when I move on, out of this world and into the next, dig my grave here, beside the Purest Branch.'[2] Nabíl-i-Qá'iní died the next morning, his heart's desire fulfilled.

When Mírzá Mihdí passed away he left a vacuum difficult to fill. Profoundly adored by his parents, brother, sister and fellow exiles, his familiar figure had disappeared from the prison floors. The spiritual gatherings where he used to share with the friends the newly-revealed Tablets had gone. In the barracks, the gloomy atmosphere was charged with grief and with memories of the times in Baghdad, Adrianople and the prison itself. He was now absent, unable to console the friends when the miseries of exile and imprisonment overcame them. The few occasions they had spent in laughter and hope, and sharing meals together, turned suddenly into periods of deep grieving and mourning. The prisoners eventually managed to regain some tranquillity with the thought that, like a guardian angel, Mírzá Mihdí was looking after them from above. Their emptiness gave way to certitude as they felt his presence at each instant and in every corner of the prison. Like the phoenix that arises from the ashes, the exiles focused on the divine promise that, thanks to him, they were to be set free from their unjust captivity, and they felt more composed. There was no reason to be sad, they believed, because Mírzá Mihdí himself had died so that they could be happy.

As seen above, the death of Mírzá Mihdí seriously affected the life of Ásíyih Khánum, titled Navváb, his mother. According to a family member:

> When the Purest Branch . . . fell from the roof and was killed, the believers were not allowed to bury him, but four soldiers came and took away the body, and

the holy family did not know for two years whether it had been thrown into the sea or what the soldiers had done with it. Naturally his mother was terribly sad and grieved at his death under such sad circumstances, and this sorrow made her so ill that it caused a disease of the heart, so that for a long time she was not able to walk about, but was obliged to sit on the bed.

However, when the Blessed Perfection said to her, 'For my sake has this come upon him, and he has borne for me a sorrow and a trouble that was coming to me,' from that day no one ever saw the mother weeping and she was always quite happy and cheerful. This was because of her faith and the strength of her spirit.[3]

As mentioned above, a few months after Mírzá Mihdí's accident the Holy Family and all the Bahá'í prisoners left the fortress. The Holy Family was moved into one rented house after another within the prison city until they were able to rent the house of Údí Khammár in 'Akká in September 1871. The house was so small that 13 people of both sexes had to occupy one room but it did provide the family a settled home for about two years.

The parents of Mírzá Mihdí experienced the pain that any parent would feel when burying a child during the parent's own lifetime. Living without him in the years following their release from imprisonment in the barracks was a heartbreaking loss that only could be ameliorated by remembering his noble life. With them remained the Purest Branch's bloodstained shirt that had to be cut from his body, a small bowl containing five smooth pebbles found in his pockets and a small but elegant walking stick. These, his only material possessions, were kept safe by the Holy Family and are now displayed in the International Archives building on Mount Carmel for pilgrims who can, through them, gain some understanding of the agonies Mírzá Mihdí suffered in the prison. Tablets in his own handwriting are also preserved at the Bahá'í World Centre.

Like any other mother suffering the loss of her child, it must have been agonising for Navváb to live without her youngest and cherished son for the next 16 years of her life. Surely Bahá'u'lláh's prayer was a strength alleviating her sorrow:

> I beseech Thee, O my Lord, by him and by his exile and his imprisonment, to send down upon such as loved him what will quiet their hearts and bless their works. Potent art Thou to do as Thou willest. No God is there but Thee, the Almighty, the Most Powerful.[4]

Bahá'u'lláh, prophet and husband, understood perfectly the depth of Navváb's pain as a mother and how she tried to reconcile her feelings of bereavement with

God's decree. To another mother who had lost a child, the Blessed Beauty revealed a Tablet full of compassion and love, explaining to her a profound spiritual truth of life:

> O thou who art the fruit of My Tree and the leaf thereof! On thee be My glory and My mercy. Let not thine heart grieve over what hath befallen thee. Wert thou to scan the pages of the Book of Life, thou wouldst, most certainly, discover that which would dissipate thy sorrows and dissolve thine anguish.
>
> Know thou, O fruit of My Tree, that the decrees of the Sovereign Ordainer, as related to fate and predestination, are of two kinds. Both are to be obeyed and accepted. The one is irrevocable, the other is, as termed by men, impending. To the former all must unreservedly submit, inasmuch as it is fixed and settled. God, however, is able to alter or repeal it. As the harm that must result from such a change will be greater than if the decree had remained unaltered, all, therefore, should willingly acquiesce in what God hath willed and confidently abide by the same.
>
> The decree that is impending, however, is such that prayer and entreaty can succeed in averting it.
>
> God grant that thou who art the fruit of My Tree, and they that are associated with thee, may be shielded from its evil consequences.
>
> Say: O God, my God! Thou hast committed into

mine hands a trust from Thee, and hast now according to the good-pleasure of Thy Will called it back to Thyself. It is not for me, who am a handmaid of Thine, to say, whence is this to me or wherefore hath it happened, inasmuch as Thou art glorified in all Thine acts, and art to be obeyed in Thy decree. Thine handmaid, O my Lord, hath set her hopes on Thy grace and bounty. Grant that she may obtain that which will draw her nigh unto Thee, and will profit her in every world of Thine. Thou art the Forgiving, the All-Bountiful. There is none other God but Thee, the Ordainer, the Ancient of Days.

Vouchsafe Thy blessings, O Lord, my God, unto them that have quaffed the wine of Thy love before the face of men, and, in spite of Thine enemies, have acknowledged Thy unity, testified to Thy oneness, and confessed their belief in that which hath made the limbs of the oppressors among Thy creatures to quake, and the flesh of the proud ones of the earth to tremble. I bear witness that Thy Sovereignty can never perish, nor Thy Will be altered. Ordain for them that have set their faces towards Thee, and for Thine handmaids that have held fast by Thy Cord, that which beseemeth the Ocean of Thy bounty and the Heaven of Thy grace.

Thou art He, O God, Who hath proclaimed Himself as the Lord of Wealth, and characterized all that serve Him as poor and needy. Even as Thou hast written: 'O ye that believe! Ye are but paupers in need

of God; but God is the All-Possessing, the All-Praised.'
Having acknowledged my poverty, and recognized
Thy wealth, suffer me not to be deprived of the glory
of Thy riches. Thou art, verily, the Supreme Protector,
the All-Knowing, the All-Wise.[5]

Navváb's profound grief was no doubt ameliorated somewhat by the marriage of her only surviving son, 'Abdu'l-Bahá, three years later, in 1873, and when she became a loving grandmother surrounded by the company of her grandchildren. Alas, her first grandson, also named Mihdí, died in 'Akká owing to the harsh conditions. Bahá'u'lláh and Navváb had eight grandchildren but only four daughters of 'Abdu'l-Bahá survived to adulthood as the unhygienic conditions of 'Akká fostered a variety of illnesses.

Bahíyyih Khánum remained unmarried. Her request to her father to devote her life to serving the Cause of God and looking after her parents and her brother was accepted. She became a close companion of her mother, helping her to run the household, looking after the pilgrims who continuously arrived from Persia and assisting her to attend to the women and children who had health problems. Bahíyyih Khánum passed away in 1932.

Navváb's last years were spent in total consecration to the Cause of God. According to her granddaughter, Ṭúbá Khánum:

Her tiny room was simple and bare – the narrow, white bed, which was also the divan in the daytime; a very small table, on which was her prayer and other holy books, her 'qalam-dán' (pen case), and leaflets for writing; there was also her rosary, sometimes a flower in a pot, and lastly an old painted box holding her other frock and her other under-garment.

Bahá'u'lláh had only two coats (made of Barak, a Persian woollen cloth); they were apt to wear out, and much of her time was spent, as I remember her, in patching and darning them and His stockings.

My eyes will always see her in her blue dress, with a white 'niqáb' [veil] on her head, and little black slippers on her tiny feet, her sweet, smiling face, and her wrapt expression, as she chanted prayers in her musical voice.

One sad day I came in from my lessons, finding many people gathered together in a troubled way. I asked 'What is the matter?'

'Your grandmother is very ill.'

I saw Bahá'u'lláh go into her room; after a time He came out; she had passed from the sadness and grief-filled days of her life on earth.

How we all wept! We missed her beautiful presence; her unfailing loving-kindness, and her perfect unselfishness had endeared her to us all.

Lovely and loving, refined and dainty, keenly intelligent, with more strength of character than of

LIFE WITHOUT MÍRZÁ MIHDÍ

physique. A strong sense of humour was also one of her many gifts.

The terrible hardships and anxieties of her life had impaired her health; she had always exerted her strength, however failing, to its utmost.[6]

In 1886, several days after falling from a height at her 'Akká home, Navváb passed away, surrounded by her husband and children. At that time Mírzá Mihdí would have been 38 years old. Navváb's strength had weakened with the passage of time. 'Abdu'l-Bahá once wrote how 'she suffered in the path of God, all of which she endured with patience and thanked God therefore and praised Him, because He had enabled her to endure afflictions for the sake of Bahá'.[7]

Shoghi Effendi wrote about the unique station of Navváb as described in the Bible:

> And, finally, 'Abdu'l-Bahá Himself in one of His remarkably significant Tablets, has borne witness not only to the exalted station of one whose 'seed shall inherit the Gentiles', whose Husband is the Lord of Hosts, but also to the sufferings endured by her who was His beloved mother. 'As to thy question concerning the 54th chapter of Isaiah,' He writes, 'This chapter refers to the Most Exalted Leaf, the mother of 'Abdu'l-Bahá. As a proof of this it is said: "For more are the children of the desolate, than the children of the

married wife." Reflect upon this statement, and then upon the following: "And thy seed shall inherit the Gentiles, and make the desolate cities to be inhabited." And truly the humiliation and reproach which she suffered in the path of God is a fact which no one can refute. For the calamities and afflictions mentioned in the whole chapter are such afflictions which she suffered in the path of God, all of which she endured with patience and thanked God therefor and praised Him, because He had enabled her to endure afflictions for the sake of Bahá. During all this time, the men and women (Covenant-breakers) persecuted her in an incomparable manner, while she was patient, God-fearing, calm, humble and contented through the favour of her Lord and by the bounty of her Creator."[8]

Her funeral was attended by many 'Akká personages, Christian and Muslim priests, and school children singing aloud poems expressing their sadness at the loss of this illustrious lady. She was buried in the local Muslim cemetery. In the International Archives building at the Bahá'í World Centre, visitors can see precious relics associated with Navváb such as her mirror, hair, handkerchief, glasses and letters.

At Navváb's death Bahá'u'lláh revealed a number of Tablets in her honour. These Tablets, quoted by the Guardian, show Him as a spouse and prophet shedding His affectionate blessings upon her as He highlights her many attributes which she clearly demonstrated throughout the long and severe years of exile and imprisonment:

'The first Spirit through which all spirits were revealed, and the first Light by which all lights shone forth, rest upon thee, O Most Exalted Leaf, thou who hast been mentioned in the Crimson Book! Thou art the one whom God created to arise and serve His own Self, and the Manifestation of His Cause, and the Day-Spring of His Revelation, and the Dawning-Place of His signs, and the Source of His commandments; and Who so aided thee that thou didst turn with thy whole being unto Him, at a time when His servants and handmaidens had turned away from His Face . . . Happy art thou, O My handmaiden, and My Leaf, and the one mentioned in My Book, and inscribed by My Pen of Glory in My Scrolls and Tablets . . . Rejoice thou, at this moment, in the most exalted Station and the All-highest Paradise, and the Abhá Horizon, inasmuch as He Who is the Lord of Names hath remembered thee. We bear witness that thou didst attain unto all good, and that God hath so exalted thee, that all honour and glory circled around thee.'

'O Navváb!' He thus, in another Tablet, addresses her, 'O Leaf that hath sprung from My Tree, and been My companion! My glory be upon thee, and My loving-kindness, and My mercy that hath surpassed all beings. We announce unto thee that which will gladden thine eye, and assure thy soul, and rejoice thine heart. Verily, thy Lord is the Compassionate, the All-Bountiful. God hath been and will be pleased with thee, and hath singled thee out for His own Self, and chosen thee from among His handmaidens to serve Him, and hath made thee the companion of His Person in the day-time and in the night-season.'

'Hear thou Me once again,' He reassures her, 'God is well-pleased with thee, as a token of His grace and a sign of His mercy. He hath made thee to be His companion in every one of His worlds, and hath nourished thee with His meeting and presence, so long as His Name, and His Remembrance, and His Kingdom, and His Empire shall endure. Happy is the handmaid that hath mentioned thee, and sought thy good-pleasure, and humbled herself before thee, and held fast unto the cord of thy love. Woe betide him that denieth thy exalted station, and the things ordained for thee from God, the Lord of all names, and him that hath turned away from thee, and rejected thy station before God, the Lord of the mighty throne.'

'O faithful ones!' Bahá'u'lláh specifically enjoins, 'Should ye visit the resting-place of the Most Exalted Leaf, who hath ascended unto the Glorious Companion, stand ye and say: 'Salutation and blessing and glory upon thee, O Holy Leaf that hath sprung from the Divine Lote-Tree! I bear witness that thou hast believed in God and in His signs, and answered His Call, and turned unto Him, and held fast unto His cord, and clung to the hem of His grace, and fled thy home in His path, and chosen to live as a stranger, out of love for His presence and in thy longing to serve Him. May God have mercy upon him that draweth nigh unto thee, and remembereth thee through the things which My Pen hath voiced in this, the most great station. We pray God that He may forgive us, and forgive them that have turned unto thee, and grant their desires, and bestow upon them, through His wondrous grace, whatever be their wish. He, verily, is the Bountiful, the Generous. Praise be to God, He Who is the Desire of all worlds; and the Beloved of all who recognize Him.'[9]

The mortal remains of the noble souls of mother and son lay in two rather unattractive cemeteries in 'Akká for many decades. It was the Guardian of the Faith, Shoghi Effendi, who provided for them their final resting place, across the bay in Haifa.

12
A Monument to the Purest Branch

In December 1939,[1] Shoghi Effendi, himself Mírzá Mihdí's great-nephew, moved the remains of the Purest Branch and those of his mother, Ásíyih Khánum, from 'Akká to a special enclosure on Mount Carmel, very close to the resting-place of Bahíyyih Khánum.

This time it was the Guardian of the Bahá'í Faith and not ordinary soldiers who carried the coffin of Mírzá Mihdí to its final resting-place. Mother, son and daughter were finally reunited forever after 70 years of physical separation, fulfilling Bahíyyih Khánum's 'cherished wish'.[2] Soon after, on 5 December 1939, Shoghi Effendi cabled to the British Bahá'ís:

REMAINS PUREST BRANCH AND ABDU'L-BAHÁ'S MOTHER PERMANENTLY LAID REST CLOSE NEIGHBOURHOOD SHRINE GREATEST HOLY LEAF HEARTS REJOICING.[3]

On the same day, a longer cable was sent to the American Bahá'ís:

A MONUMENT TO THE PUREST BRANCH

BLESSED REMAINS PUREST BRANCH AND MASTER'S MOTHER SAFELY TRANSFERRED HALLOWED PRECINCTS SHRINES MOUNT CARMEL. LONG INFLICTED HUMILIATION WIPED AWAY. MACHINATIONS COVENANT-BREAKERS FRUSTRATE PLAN DEFEATED. CHERISHED WISH GREATEST HOLY LEAF FULFILLED. SISTER BROTHER MOTHER WIFE ABDU'L-BAHÁ REUNITED ONE SPOT DESIGNED CONSTITUTE FOCAL CENTRE BAHÁ'Í ADMINISTRATIVE INSTITUTIONS AT FAITH'S WORLD CENTRE. SHARE JOYFUL NEWS ENTIRE BODY AMERICAN BELIEVERS. – SHOGHI RABBANI[4]

On 26 December Shoghi Effendi again cabled the American Bahá'ís:

CHRISTMAS EVE BELOVED REMAINS PUREST BRANCH AND MASTER'S MOTHER LAID IN STATE BÁB'S HOLY TOMB. CHRISTMAS DAY ENTRUSTED CARMEL'S SACRED SOIL. CEREMONY PRESENCE REPRESENTATIVES NEAR EASTERN BELIEVERS PROFOUNDLY MOVING. IMPELLED ASSOCIATE AMERICA'S MOMENTOUS SEVEN-YEAR ENTERPRISE IMPERISHABLE MEMORY THESE TWO HOLY SOULS WHO NEXT TWIN FOUNDERS FAITH AND PERFECT EXEMPLAR TOWER TOGETHER WITH GREATEST HOLY LEAF ABOVE ENTIRE CONCOURSE FAITHFUL. REJOICE PRIVILEGE PLEDGE THOUSAND POUNDS MY CONTRIBUTION BAHIYYIH KHANUM FUND DESIGNED INAUGURATION FINAL DRIVE ENSURE PLACING CONTRACT NEXT APRIL

LAST REMAINING STAGE CONSTRUCTION MASHRIQU'L-ADHKAR. TIME PRESSING OPPORTUNITY PRICELESS POTENT AID PROVIDENTIALLY PROMISED UNFAILING. – SHOGHI RABBANI[5]

Over the graves of Mírzá Mihdí, Navváb and the Greatest Holy Leaf he built beautiful marble monuments for 'these three incomparably precious souls who, next to the three Central Figures of our Faith, tower in rank above the vast multitude of the heroes, Letters, martyrs, hands, teachers and administrators of the Cause of Bahá'u'lláh'.[6]

The monuments for Mírzá Mihdí and his mother are identical, the dome of each being supported by seven pillars.

Shortly after the reinterment of Mírzá Mihdí and his mother, on 21 December 1939, Shoghi Effendi wrote a significant letter, entitled 'The Spiritual Potencies of that Consecrated Spot', describing the spiritual significance of this event and of this sacred place:

> The Purest Branch, the martyred son, the companion, and amanuensis of Bahá'u'lláh, that pious and holy youth, who in the darkest days of Bahá'u'lláh's incarceration in the barracks of 'Akká entreated, on his death-bed, his Father to accept him as a ransom for those of His loved ones who yearned for, but were unable to attain, His presence, and the saintly mother

of 'Abdu'l-Bahá, surnamed Navváb by Bahá'u'lláh, and the first recipient of the honoured and familiar title of 'the Most Exalted Leaf', separated in death above half a century, and forced to suffer the humiliation of an alien burial-ground, are now at long last reunited with the Greatest Holy Leaf with whom they had so abundantly shared the tribulations of one of the most distressing episodes of the Heroic Age of the Faith of Bahá'u'lláh. Avenged, eternally safeguarded, befittingly glorified, they repose embosomed in the heart of Carmel, hidden beneath its sacred soil, interred in one single spot, lying beneath the shadow of the twin holy Tombs, and facing across the bay, on an eminence of unequalled loveliness and beauty, the silver-city of 'Akká, the Point of Adoration of the entire Bahá'í world, and the Door of Hope for all mankind. 'Haste thee, O Carmel!' thus proclaims the Pen of Bahá'u'lláh, 'for lo, the light of the countenance of God, the Ruler of the Kingdom of Names and Fashioner of the heavens, hath been lifted upon thee.' 'Rejoice, for God hath in this Day established upon thee His throne, hath made thee the dawning-place of His signs and the day-spring of the evidences of His Revelation . . .'

For it must be clearly understood, nor can it be sufficiently emphasized, that the conjunction of the resting-place of the Greatest Holy Leaf with those of her brother and mother incalculably reinforces the spiritual potencies of that consecrated Spot which, under the wings of the Báb's overshadowing Sepulchre, and in the vicinity of the future Ma<u>sh</u>riqu'l-A<u>dh</u>kár, which will be reared on its flank, is destined to evolve into the focal centre of those world-shaking, world-embracing, world-directing administrative institutions, ordained by Bahá'u'lláh and anticipated by 'Abdu'l-Bahá, and which are to function in consonance with the principles that govern the twin institutions of the Guardianship and the Universal House of Justice. Then, and then only, will this momentous prophecy which illuminates the concluding passages of the Tablet of Carmel be fulfilled: 'Ere long will God sail His Ark upon thee (Carmel), and will manifest the people of Bahá who have been mentioned in the Book of Names.'[7]

The Guardian later wrote:

The conjunction of these three resting-places, under the shadow of the Báb's own Tomb, embosomed in the heart of Carmel, facing the snow-white city across the bay of 'Akká, the Qiblih of the Bahá'í world, set in a garden of exquisite beauty, reinforces, if we would correctly estimate its significance, the spiritual potencies of a spot, designated by Bahá'u'lláh Himself the seat of God's throne. It marks, too, a further milestone in the road leading eventually to the establishment of that permanent world Administrative Centre of the future Bahá'í Commonwealth, destined never to

The monument marking the resting place of the Greatest Holy Leaf, circa 1932

The monument over the grave of the Greatest Holy Leaf

Monuments to Mírzá Mihdí and Navváb

Bronze plaque on the monument to Mírzá Mihdí

Monuments to Mírzá Mihdí and Navváb

Today, Bahá'í youth all over the world, inspired by the service and sacrifice of the Purest Branch, are studying the teachings of Bahá'u'lláh, building their capacity and arising in sacrificial service to their communities

be separated from, and to function in the proximity of, the Spiritual Centre of that Faith, in a land already revered and held sacred alike by the adherents of three of the world's outstanding religious systems.[8]

For joy, the Hill of God [Mount Carmel] is stirred at so high an honour, and for this most great bestowal the mountain of the Lord is in rapture and ecstasy.[9]

Shoghi Effendi also remarked on the 'association of the First Mashriqu'l-Adhkár of the West with the hallowed memories of the Purest Branch and of 'Abdu'l-Bahá's mother'.[10]

Mother and brother resting together, with Bahíyyih Khánum lying a few metres away near the wife of 'Abdu'l-Bahá, Munírih Khánum, and 'Abdu'l-Bahá Himself buried within walking distance, the Holy Family was reunited around the Báb's Shrine, fulfilling the prophecy of the Tablet of Carmel revealed nearly half a century before.

The landscape was the antithesis of the Most Great Prison. The Purest Branch and the Most Exalted Leaf now lay within a beautiful oval garden, ever attended by tall, slender, watch-guard trees standing like heavenly sentinels; chirping birds day and night cheering the environs, declaring that this is death but also life; crowned by the open sky and caressed by the gentle breezes meandering between the sea and the mountain;

colourful flowers replacing the squalid prison walls; stars and lighting illuminating the precinct, marking the demise of the obscurity of the ghastly barracks; and positioned with a bird's-eye, panoramic view of the city of Haifa and the Most Great Prison across the bay, reminding us, as in the best of stories, that freedom shall prevail over oppression. As God had promised to the wife of the Lord of Hosts in the Bible, that is, to Navváb, 'great shall be the peace of thy children',[11] prophesying that one day her grave would be covered with colourful gems and sapphires.[12]

While in Mírzá Mihdí's time a handful of believers from Iran and Iraq managed to come to the Holy Land, today some four thousand Bahá'í pilgrims arrive each year from all over the world to visit the Shrines of Bahá'u'lláh and the Báb. The visitors have the honour of visiting the resting-place of Mírzá Mihdí and his cell in the barracks as well as the place where the tragic accident took place, and remembering his precious life of dedicated service to the Blessed Beauty, and calling to mind their predecessors, the early and devoted Persian pilgrims, who were the first permitted to enter the presence of Bahá'u'lláh owing to the sacrifice of the Purest Branch.

13

The Ode of the Dove

We will probably never understand why Mírzá Mihdí had five little stones in his pockets at the time of his death. There were four oval stones – three white and one grey – and one beige stone with a spike. All five stones could be held in one hand.

Was there any spiritual significance to them? Were they, as suggested by Kiser Barnes,[1] connected to the five pebbles that the small David collected from a stream to use in his simple slingshot to fight with Goliath, the giant, an incident much celebrated in biblical narratives as the triumph of goodness over evil? Were they part of a local juggling game used in some cultures to overcome boredom? Were the pebbles perhaps associated with powerful memories in Mírzá Mihdí's challenging life?

Who might have brought these pebbles to him and for what purpose are two other enigmas. Were these stones brought by a pilgrim from a holy place? Might they have been a gift from a cousin, a friend, his grandmother or aunt when he left Tehran to join his parents after a separation of seven years? Or perhaps they were merely purchased at the local market for his own pleasure with whatever meagre money he could afford. Would it be that he used them like 'worry beads', something to turn over and over in his hands; or as simple prayer beads, to count the recitations of a prayer or verse?

Irrespective of whether Mírzá Mihdí acquired the pebbles himself or received them as a gift, where did they come from? Perhaps from the bucolic forest of Núr, the noisy Tehran streets, the provincial Baghdad landscape or from the idyllic Adrianople scenery where he might have made many friends? Or did they come from the shores of the Caspian, the Black, the Marmara or the Mediterranean seas, whose waters he had traversed in powerful steamers and sailing ships and gave him solace and a backdrop for reflection and contemplation in his unsettled residence? Or were they from the 'Akká beach, within sight but unreachable from Mírzá Mihdí's prison cell, a reminder that life went on outside the ugly walls, beyond the land gate, in what was to him a forbidden world?

Most likely we will never know the mystery and significance of those five small stones. All we can say is that those smooth pebbles, like priceless gems, were highly treasured by Mírzá Mihdí and accompanied him in his last devotions before he met his end. Interestingly, his resting place is surrounded now by innumerable beautiful white rounded pebbles, as if the landscape were returning thousandfold his most treasured possessions.

Yet it is Mírzá Mihdí's recitation of the Ode of the

THE ODE OF THE DOVE

Dove (Qaṣídiy-i-Varqá'íyyih) in the last moments of his life that tells us more about him than his meagre earthly possessions can. This celebrated 127-verse poem of Bahá'u'lláh, revealed when Mírzá Mihdí was still living in Tehran, gives voice to Bahá'u'lláh's sorrows in the Cause of God. It is presented as a dialogue between Bahá'u'lláh and the Maid of Heaven, representing the Spirit of God. The ode was revealed during Bahá'u'lláh's two-year withdrawal into the mountains of Kurdistan, north of Baghdad. Shoghi Effendi explained the history of the poem in which the Blessed Beauty identified Himself as the Dove:

> Amazed by the profundity of His insight and the compass of His understanding, they [the Islamic scholars in Kurdistan] were impelled to seek from Him what they considered to be a conclusive and final evidence of the unique power and knowledge which He now appeared in their eyes to possess. 'No one among the mystics, the wise, and the learned,' they claimed, while requesting this further favour from Him, 'has hitherto proved himself capable of writing a poem in a rhyme and metre identical with that of the longer of the two odes, entitled Qaṣídiy-i-Tá'íyyih composed by Ibn-i-Faríd. We beg you to write for us a poem in that same metre and rhyme.' This request was complied with, and no less than two thousand verses, in exactly the manner they had specified, were dictated by Him, out

> of which He selected one hundred and twenty-seven, which He permitted them to keep, deeming the subject matter of the rest premature and unsuitable to the needs of the times. It is these same one hundred and twenty-seven verses that constitute the Qaṣídiy-i-Varqá'íyyih, so familiar to, and widely circulated amongst, His Arabic speaking followers.
>
> Such was their reaction to this marvellous demonstration of the sagacity and genius of Bahá'u'lláh that they unanimously acknowledged every single verse of that poem to be endowed with a force, beauty and power far surpassing anything contained in either the major or minor odes composed by that celebrated poet.[2]

The Ode of the Dove is certainly a captivating text, not only for its mystical themes but also for the superior literary quality of its Arabic, framed with rhythms and a melodious cadence that enraptures the soul when chanted. Given that Arabic was not his first language, Mírzá Mihdí must have been highly literate and fluent in that language to be able to understand a text which is very difficult for ordinary readers to comprehend. According to Adib Taherzadeh, 'The words He [Bahá'u'lláh] has used in this poem are very rich in their meanings and as they blend together, they produce a divine orchestra of spiritual melodies.'[3] The Ode of the Dove is the same Tablet that moved Badí', then a troubled teenager, to accept, in tears, the Faith of Bahá'u'lláh and prompted him to undertake the long journey to visit the Blessed Beauty.

Here the Manifestation of God expands on His afflictions and His struggles to advance the Cause of God in the face of numerous tests and obstacles. As mentioned above, the Ode of the Dove contains very poignant verses able to touch every sensitive heart:

> Noah's flood is but the measure of the tears I have shed, and Abraham's fire an ebullition of My soul. Jacob's grief is but a reflection of My sorrows, and Job's afflictions a fraction of my calamity.[4]

One wonders whether Mírzá Mihdí's recitation of the Ode of the Dove was a spiritual premonition and a preparation for the accident and injuries that over the following 22 hours caused such an agonizing death. All the chroniclers of that time paid tribute to his composure as he suffered what must have been terrible pain. To the very moment of his death Mírzá Mihdí demonstrated that he was a Branch of the Tree of God, not only because of his lineage but also for what he made of himself by his title, the Purest Branch.

We will never know exactly how Mírzá Mihdí failed to notice the open skylight other than that he was concentrating on his devotions and that the accident happened 'in the gathering darkness'.[5] Certainly the roof was an area that had to be treated with care. The skylight had no protective guard around it and there were no fences or walls around the roof edge other than a perimetric brick border. However, Mírzá Mihdí knew the space very well as he had visited the roof continually over a period of two years and was well aware of the dangers. According to the historian Hasan Balyuzi and based on Mírzá Mihdí's own testimony, 'he had always counted his steps to that skylight but on that evening had forgotten to do so'.[6] Adib Taherzadeh relates that Mírzá Mihdí fell as he 'paced along that familiar space wrapped in his customary meditations with his eyes closed . . .'[7] The exiles' cook recalled that 'As he [Mírzá Mihdí] was pacing in a state of prayer, attracted to the Kingdom of Abhá, with his head turned upwards, he fell through the skylight down on some hard objects.'[8] And of those tragic circumstances Shoghi Effendi wrote, 'He was pacing the roof of the barracks in the twilight, one evening, wrapped in his customary devotions, when he fell through the unguarded skylight onto a wooden crate, standing on the floor beneath, which pierced his ribs . . .'[9]

The pain from the impact of his body on the stone surface ten metres below must have been excruciating.

Following the collapse of the powerful Ottoman Empire, the British captured 'Akká in 1918 and eventually, in the 1930s, transformed the barracks into a prison for Jewish activists. In 1921, after a series of bloody wars of secession and conflicts with its neighbours, Turkey's territory was reduced to a small republic and the Sultanate abolished.

The open skylight that took Mírzá Mihdí's life disappeared years later when the authorities of the British Mandate altered the prison roof to increase security. Interestingly, the story of the skylight is not related in the notes of a pilgrim visiting the prison in 1919,[10] although a later pilgrim did mention it in a letter written in 1925.[11]

A pilgrim group visiting 1919 was guided through the prison-city by one of the Bahá'í prisoners who had witnessed Mírzá Mihdí's accident. One of the pilgrims recorded what he saw and, no doubt, what he learned from the guide:

> In the 'most great prison' cell overlooking the sea, with nineteen rafters and three large cross beams, Bahá'u'lláh was confined for two years. A stone cell without bed or chair, the hard stone floor its only resting place . . . By a little barred window, Bahá'u'lláh used to stand and show himself to hundreds of pilgrims a mile away. These devoted followers, who left family and home in far-away Persia, crossed sand deserts on foot in the weltering sun with scanty food, for just one look of recognition, one hand wave of acknowledgement from 'Him whom God would manifest' . . . But to continue on our way, we passed into

> another similar room in which thirteen members of the household lived, and adjoining, the room which the Purest Branch occupied, the brother of 'Abdu'l-Bahá. He died in this room . . .[12]

As mentioned above, by the time of these pilgrimages, 'Akká was no longer part of the Ottoman Empire. Remember that soon after Bahá'u'lláh arrived in 'Akká as a prisoner, He predicted the Sultan's downfall and the loss of his vast territories. The Sultan himself was deposed, put in prison and died, apparently assassinated in June 1876. Bahá'u'lláh had prophesied this in the Súriy-i-Ra'ís, a Tablet addressed to the Ottoman prime minister just as the exiles were being moved from Adrianople to Gallipoli en route to 'Akká:

> The day is approaching when the Land of Mystery [Adrianople] and what is beside it shall be changed, and shall pass out of the hands of the King, and commotions shall appear, and the voice of lamentation shall be raised, and the evidences of mischief shall be revealed on all sides, and confusion shall spread by reason of that which hath befallen these captives at the hands of the hosts of oppression.[13]

The unusual way that 'Akká eventually passed from Turkish to British hands was explained many years later by Wellesley Tudor Pole:

Before the fall of Haifa, 'Abdu'l-Bahá was discussing the British campaign with a few of His followers in His garden one day. He then predicted that, contrary to the general expectation, the taking of Haifa and the walled town of 'Akká would come about almost without bloodshed. This prediction was verified by the facts. He also stated that the Turks would surrender 'Akká (supposed to be impregnable) to two unarmed British soldiers. The resultant facts so far as I was able to gather them were as follows: –

Subsequent to the entry of our troops into Haifa, the front line was pushed forward half-way across the Bay of 'Akká, and outposts were placed in position on the sands of the Bay some four miles from 'Akká itself. 'Akká, as a fortified and walled town, was believed to be filled with Turkish troops at this time. Very early one morning two British Army Service soldiers, who had lost their bearings in the night, found themselves at the gates of 'Akká, believing erroneously that the town was already in British hands. However, the Turkish rearguard troops had been secretly evacuated only eight hours earlier, and the Mayor of the town, seeing British soldiers outside the gates, came down and presented them with the keys of the town in token of surrender! It is credibly stated that the dismayed Tommies, being unarmed, dropped the keys and made post haste for the British lines![14]

MÍRZÁ MIHDÍ

By that time the demographics had changed and Palestine was becoming increasingly populated by Jewish people from all parts of the world. By 1948 the State of Israel was formed, extending its sovereignty to 'Akká.

By 2003, and despite its architectural value, the citadel complex had deteriorated and was in a precarious condition. After careful research into Ottoman and British historical records, the whole citadel was renovated and restored to its original character. The research uncovered important information about different aspects of the citadel. For instance, it was found that, before Bahá'u'lláh's arrival, the barracks had been a residential compound for high-ranking officers of the Ottoman army. The building had been abandoned, and was almost uninhabitable, when the Holy Family arrived in 1868.

Surprisingly, during the renovation, a previously unknown German aerial photograph taken in 1917 and showing the exact location of the skylight was unearthed, facilitating the reinstallation of the feature. The original citadel has been described as having an outer section that included a 'verandah (above which was the skylight), a kitchen, latrines, a mezzanine, and a biruni' – a room Bahá'u'lláh used to receive His visitors. The eastern side faced the courtyard with three open arches bounded by pairs of columns serving as balcony openings (now filled in). Other Baha'is lived elsewhere in the citadel.[15]

The exact place where Mírzá Mihdí fell, and the original stone floor below the skylight, were thereby clearly identified and subsequently roped off, to signify the space as a special place for pilgrims, where they can revere his memory, say prayers on his behalf and remember his illustrious life in Bahá'í history.

When the site was restored, the skylight was left unguarded, as in its original form. Acting like an open window to the sky, the skylight enabled the sun once again to stream its light on this tragic spot during daytime while at night the stars keep a permanent vigil on it.

14

Epilogue

Mírzá Mihdí was the Purest Branch not only by title but by character. He was an 'Aghsán', that is, a branch from Bahá'u'lláh's tree, attracting attention and respect from the believers, and Bahá'u'lláh's second oldest son surviving to adulthood. His benevolent and delicate nature is reflected in the two photographs of him that have come to us, both taken in Adrianople. These show a tender face adorned by a simple, short white turban and long hair, his face radiating spiritual meekness. Had he lived to an older age, humanity would have received a great blessing. But Mírzá Mihdí was a unique creation, a divine gift that was, inscrutably and suddenly, exchanged by his Creator for other gifts as precious as his soul: the unification of the human race, the happiness of the Bahá'ís and the liberation of their Lord.

It appears that during His life, Bahá'u'lláh associated the quality of purity with only two believers: Mírzá Mihdí and Ṭáhirih, the most outstanding woman in the Bábí dispensation, who was given this title meaning 'the Pure One' by the Báb. We know that Mírzá Mihdí's title is the Purest Branch or the Most

Pure Branch, Ghuṣn-i-Aṭhar (Ghuṣnu'lláhu'l-Aṭhar). The root *aṭhar* أطهر in Arabic is primarily translated as 'pure' and can alternatively be rendered as 'chaste', 'clean' or 'immaculate', as in Ṭáhirih the Pure One or the Chaste One. Thus, Mírzá Mihdí's title is indicative of the unsullied character that he exemplified as a Bahá'í aligned to Bahá'u'lláh's teachings.

While most believers are given a lifetime to develop their spiritual qualities and attain true maturity, Mírzá Mihdí was able in only one decade to demonstrate the excellence of his being: he reached such perfection through ten years of devoted service to his father. Bahá'í chroniclers revealed Mírzá Mihdí's fine attributes in a number of snapshot-like references in their narratives. At one time we see him being ferried with Bahá'u'lláh and 'Abdu'l-Bahá across the Tigris to reach the Riḍván Garden; at another he is sending sweets to a believer in prison. He is seen attending an interview of Bahá'u'lláh with another believer and, on other occasions, comforting the exiles in their tribulations. Mírzá Mihdí, as part of his role as an amanuensis, had the inestimable privilege of continuously listening and writing down the Word of God in its original purity as it was revealed by the Blessed Beauty. Mírzá Mihdí grew to spiritual maturity more quickly than he grew to physical adulthood. Owing to his divine lineage and qualities, he established himself among the believers as a much-loved 'Branch of God'. He was not only a blood descendant but also a true spiritual son of his father, just as 'Abdu'l-Bahá wrote, 'The child is the secret essence of its sire'.[1]

Mírzá Mihdí's story is an illuminating one for all the youth of the world. Here is a young man who was deprived of many of the comforts and pleasures that life brings to an average young person. Although born into what was at the time an aristocratic family, for the sake of God, he experienced deprivations, persecution and grew up besieged by religious prejudice and hatred. Removed at the age of four from his parents and siblings during seven significant developmental years of his life, he was also deprived of ordinary childhood experiences of laughter, playmates and fun. Belonging to a family whose fate was marked by continual banishments, Mírzá Mihdí was never able to settle in one place. For him and his family, life in Baghdad, Constantinople and Adrianople was not easy from a material perspective. There was constant uncertainty about their next destination and they were forced to leave what are now three distinct countries – Iran, Iraq and Turkey – for a fourth, Israel. With every move, each new habitation had to be transformed very quickly into a home, including the prison of 'Akká.

In an era when most young men of his age married and became apprentices in a trade that would help them raise a family, Mírzá Mihdí thought only of serving his father and his faith. Certainly, he was a youth who spent much of his time contemplating the Word of God. Today we see young people engrossed in their sophisticated playthings whereas Mírzá Mihdí only had five smooth stones for recreation.

And to add to the afflictions he suffered during his short existence, life was taken from him in a terrible accident at the young age of 22 during the second year of his imprisonment. His mishap occurred whilst he was in a state of prayer, unlike so many of the controversial accidents that youth suffer these days. The burial itself was conducted by strangers and his grave covered by foreign dust.

Yet Mírzá Mihdí had a life filled with spiritual meaning. His suffering poses questions for which no clear answers may exist. We can reflect on the mystery of sacrifice of one who was so close spiritually, and physically, to the Manifestation of God. Christ's words might explain the purpose of Mírzá Mihdí's sacrifice: 'Greater love hath no man than this, that a man lay down his life for his friends.'[2]

The mystery of Mírzá Mihdí's sacrifice was that, given the choice of living, his final plea to die that the happiness of the Bahá'ís might be achieved was not only accepted but extended to be the leaven to achieve the unification of all humankind. In the past, a captive king was released only after the payment of a huge ransom. In like manner, the world, a captive to its disunity, required a ransom. As Baharieh Ma'ani asserts, 'Mírzá Mihdí was the worthy candidate for the purpose.'³ In biblical terms, he is the lamb sacrificed by Abraham in place of the sacrifice of His son.⁴ In religious history, God had always demanded a hefty personal and physical sacrifice from His prophets, commensurate with their grandeur. Jesus and the Báb sacrificed themselves, in Muhammad's dispensation that sacrifice is represented by His grandson Ḥusayn, while in the Bahá'í Faith, the Prophet's son – as in Abraham's story – became the instrument of redemption. Bahá'u'lláh's entreaty for martyrdom was an unmet yearning, as revealed in this dialogue in which He converses with His innermost self:

> My blood, at all times, addresseth me saying: 'O Thou Who art the Image of the Most Merciful! How long will it be ere Thou riddest me of the captivity of this world, and deliverest me from the bondage of this life? Didst Thou not promise me that Thou shalt dye the earth with me, and sprinkle me on the faces of the inmates of Thy Paradise?' To this I make reply: 'Be thou patient and quiet thyself. The things thou desirest can last but an hour. As to me, however, I quaff continually in the path of God the cup of His decree, and wish not that the ruling of His will should cease to operate, or that the woes I suffer for the sake of my Lord, the Most Exalted, the All-Glorious, should be ended. Seek thou my wish and forsake thine own. Thy bondage is not

for my protection, but to enable me to sustain successive tribulations, and to prepare me for the trials that must needs repeatedly assail me. Perish that lover who discerneth between the pleasant and the poisonous in his love for his beloved! Be thou satisfied with what God hath destined for thee. He, verily, ruleth over thee as He willeth and pleaseth. No God is there but Him, the Inaccessible, the Most High.'[5]

Mírzá Mihdí was also the sacrifice of a family that had thus far given up so much in the path of God. One might ask himself why Providence had immersed the Holy Family in the 'bitter grief of a sudden tragedy'.[6] What wisdom was hidden behind this misfortune that could help soothe his parents' grief? As Jay Neugeboren in *An Orphan's Tale* laments:

> A wife who loses a husband is called a widow. A husband who loses a wife is called a widower. A child who loses his parents is called an orphan. But in Yiddish they say there is no word for a parent who loses a child, that's how awful the loss is![7]

Why does God take the life of a youth so prematurely? In consoling two parents on the death of their young son, and perhaps parallelling their loss with that of His own brother, 'Abdu'l-Bahá provided this comforting answer:

> It is as if a kind gardener transferreth a fresh and tender shrub from a confined place to a wide open area. This transfer is not the cause of the withering, the lessening or the destruction of that shrub; nay, on the contrary, it maketh it to grow and thrive, acquire freshness and delicacy, become green and bear fruit. This hidden secret is well known to the gardener, but those souls who are unaware of this bounty suppose that the gardener, in his anger and wrath, hath uprooted the shrub. Yet to those who are aware, this concealed fact is manifest, and this predestined decree is considered a bounty. Do not feel grieved or disconsolate, therefore, at the ascension of that bird of faithfulness; nay, under all circumstances pray for that youth, supplicating for him forgiveness and the elevation of his station.[8]

Bahá'u'lláh referred to Mírzá Mihdí as the 'trust of God and His treasure in this land'.[9] A trust is something entrusted to a person to take care of, for example, 'each member of the human race is born into the world as a trust of the whole.'[10] How wonderful, therefore, it is that we Bahá'ís have been made custodians of such an incomparable trust. The implications of such a binding relationship make us spiritual trustees. However, such an obligation goes further than looking after Mírzá Mihdí's sacred remains, now under the direct care of the Universal House of Justice. It is also about preserving his memory and keeping it alive by living his life in our daily lives. Whenever we suffer personal hardship for the sake of the Cause of God, let us first ensure the happiness of those who are also suffering.

Mírzá Mihdí was also God's 'treasure'. He was indeed a precious asset to Him and to the world. He was a treasure by virtue of his own spiritual qualities, for his inestimable value as a ransom for the liberation of the King of Kings, for the Prophet's blood running through his veins, and for being 'created by the light of Bahá'.[11] An incalculable treasure, he was a priceless gift that the Divinity made manifest to humanity for a very limited time and under exceptional circumstances. On the landscape of history, his life was that window which from time to time Providence opens to share God's treasures, His chosen ones. Thus does God remind us that He is the All-Possessing and that His riches, both spiritual and material, cannot be compared to the material objects and wealth that humans too often value. Mírzá Mihdí was God's cherished treasure, one who was so loved that he was quickly returned to his Creator.

Shoghi Effendi once wrote, 'The time has come for the friends . . . to think not as to how they should serve the Cause, but how the Cause should be served.'[12] Mírzá Mihdí, at a tender age, certainly recognized this principle, as evidenced in the hours following his accident. Here is a youth who, when asked by his omnipotent father what he wished for and given the possibility of being healed, immediately thought of the most pressing need of the Cause of God, which was for 'the believers to be admitted to see their Lord',[13] and that Bahá'u'lláh be released from prison. Mírzá Mihdí's response was instantaneous and compelling, as if he had been seriously thinking about this for a long time. He put the needs of the Faith first and the result was immediate: 'Soon after the martyrdom of the Purest Branch many restrictions in the barracks were relaxed and several believers who were longing to attain the presence of Bahá'u'lláh did so,' wrote Adib Taherzadeh.[14] Within a few months, Bahá'u'lláh and His family were moved out of the barracks into accommodation within the city of 'Akká and a few years later Bahá'u'lláh left 'Akká altogether and moved into the countryside.

Mírzá Mihdí's sacrifice reminds us of Bahá'u'lláh's words of promise for those who perform pure and goodly deeds:

> One righteous act is endowed with a potency that can so elevate the dust as to cause it to pass beyond the heaven of heavens. It can tear every bond asunder, and hath the power to restore the force that hath spent itself and vanished . . .[15]

From the barracks, Bahá'u'lláh, Head of the Bahá'í Faith, guided and led the believers who were by then established mainly in Iran, the Ottoman Empire, Russia and elsewhere. Today, as promised by Bahá'u'lláh in His Tablet of Carmel – 'Ere long will God sail His Ark upon thee [Carmel], and will manifest the people of Bahá who have been mentioned in the Book of Names'[16] – the Bahá'í World Centre is established in Haifa, across the bay from 'Akká. It comprises a large number of buildings and properties and the Faith itself is established in virtually every country and in many dependent territories and overseas departments of countries.[17] Hence the functions of the Head of the Faith, now vested in the Universal House of Justice, have multiplied and with that the number of believers serving as volunteer workers in the Holy Land, particularly youth, has increased. These youth, coming from every continent of the globe, are reminiscent of Mírzá Mihdí and of the handful of youth who lived in the barracks serving their Lord. While Mírzá Mihdí's single task was to hear and record the voice of revelation, the young believers serving in the Holy Land today are engaged in a multitude of tasks, from office workers, to gardeners, from security officers to janitors. More importantly, when they visit the barracks where he fell to his death or his beautiful mausoleum in the Monument Gardens, or when they read the testimonies to his exalted station issued from Bahá'u'lláh's pen, they find in Mírzá Mihdí an inspiring example of service, dedication and character worth emulating.

MÍRZÁ MIHDÍ

Mírzá Mihdí's service has been highlighted by the Universal House of Justice in the context of the amazing capacities that Bahá'í youth have exhibited since the inception of the Faith:

> From the very beginning of the Bahá'í Era, youth have played a vital part in the promulgation of God's Revelation. The Báb Himself was but twenty-five years old when He declared His Mission, while many of the Letters of the Living were even younger. The Master, as a very young man, was called upon to shoulder heavy responsibilities in the service of His Father in Iraq and Turkey; and His brother, the Purest Branch, yielded up his life to God in the Most Great Prison at the age of twenty-two that the servants of God might 'be quickened, and all that dwell on earth be united'. Shoghi Effendi was a student at Oxford when called to the throne of his Guardianship, and many of the Knights of Bahá'u'lláh, who won imperishable fame during the Ten Year Crusade, were young people. Let it, therefore, never be imagined that youth must await their years of maturity before they can render invaluable services to the Cause of God.[18]

Countless souls of this ephemeral world have set their ambitions on earthly possessions and vanished. No fruit of them has remained, no hint, no symbol, no trace, not even an indication of their identity.

EPILOGUE

Their opportunity to use their ability to co-create history was lost. Not so for Mírzá Mihdí who laid down his humble life at the Threshold of God, who shone forth like a beacon of light in the endless heavens of ancient glory, shedding his splendour throughout all the breadth of time. The Purest Branch is a fleeting star in the annals of Bahá'í history. Fleeting stars are so luminous and sparkling that they are visible to any discerning eye, although their trajectories are short and transient. Emerging from deep space, they are celestial objects that graciously illumine us with their glare and meteoritic power, drawing the hearts and minds of all, expanding our thirst for the immensity of the unknown.

From time immemorial people have been attracted to fleeting stars for mysterious reasons. They are considered talismans of good fortune, omens gleaming brightly from the endless sky of eternal grace, divine oracles guiding us at seemingly unconquerable crossroads, moments that we await to embellish a dark night, extra-terrestrial messengers reminding us that we are not alone in this immense cosmos, metaphors emanating the secrets of life and death, and fossilized remains bearing testimony of the liveliness of this universe despite its profound darkness. Mírzá Mihdí's life was also one of profound significance, adding new meaning to our existence: that life can be short and beautiful; that it is possible to manifest constructive resilience in the most appalling circumstances; that the sea of life can be implacable but offer a haven of peace; and that the veil obscuring the mystery of death can be rent asunder at any moment and still be embraced with unalloyed love. And when death dawns upon us, without any hint of hesitation, we plunge ourselves into realms unknown to the mortal eye. Like the fleeting stars, impelled by inescapable physical forces and in the most thrilling period of their existence, perish, the life of the Purest Branch ended abruptly, inexorably linked to his divine provenance. At a more philosophical level, Mírzá Mihdí's story clearly demonstrates that the infamies of humanity somehow continue despite human enlightenment: imprisonment, oppression, desolation, tyranny, malice, sedition and deceit. And yet, this extraordinary life, which emanated such an abundance of dazzling light, comforts us with hope – hope that the more powerful forces of joy, compassion, generosity, love and purity sit at the core of the human heart. As with the fleeting stars, our significance is not connected to the duration of our earthly existence but rather to the grace we bring to the lives of others. What matters is how brightly we shine on the spiritual firmament of life despite suffering, and how pleasantly we will be remembered once we are gone.

* * *

EPILOGUE

These days, Bahá'í pilgrims to the Holy Land lodge in hotels and not in caves, they travel in planes and not on foot, their travelling time will take a few hours rather than the five-month journey from Persia on the dusty routes of the old Silk Road, the highways of the past. They are regarded as guests of the Universal House of Justice and welcomed with much love, as Bahá'u'lláh welcomed pilgrims Himself. They will not worry about medical facilities because the land of Palestine, now Israel, is an advanced and modern country offering high standards of care and comfort to the visitor. No more prison guards but courteous and well-trained tourist guides smile at sightseers. No longer a poorly-educated and a hostile population but warm citizens who welcome the visitors. Electric lights and running water are everywhere, communication with the rest of the world is instantaneous through the Internet, and civil human liberties such as religious freedom and the proscription against imprisoning children and youth indefinitely are enforced.

Pilgrims visiting the empty barracks hear neither the noise of children playing nor the chants of devotion resounding on the solid stone structure. The women's conversations as they battled through the arduous chores and the talk of the elderly revisiting nostalgically their past are missing. But the modern pilgrim can evoke the joy of the exiles when they spotted a new pilgrim approaching from the unreachable outside world and perhaps share the emotions felt by the prisoners at news from the motherland ushered, with much caution, in through the prison walls. The modern pilgrim will take in as much as possible the evocative atmosphere with reverence, will recreate the lives of the spiritual ancestors with much respect, and approach the barracks as a hallowed spot that once housed God's Manifestation.

The courtyard and its filthy pool have given way to archaeological excavations while the whole citadel has been renovated to museum standards, the owls, flies and rats gone with the stench of the city. The barracks themselves have become a place of interest not only to Bahá'ís but also to tourists from all over the world, attracted to the history of Israel.

As they walk through the old barracks, pilgrims will take time to explore the cells, imagining the spaces as they were in Bahá'u'lláh's time. And they will recall the suffering of those who lived here for more than two years and try to understand those believers patiently surviving through each day in the worst conditions but, ironically, happy because they were living behind bars with the Manifestation of God and had the blessing of knowing His great creation, the Purest Branch.

Appendix

The Burial of the Purest Branch and the Mother of 'Abdu'l-Bahá

by Rúḥíyyih Rabbani[1]

The garden is dark. Twilight has fallen on Mount Carmel and the veils of dusk have deepened over the bay of 'Akká. A group of men stand waiting by the gate, beneath the steps. Suddenly there is a stir, the gardener runs to illumine the entrance and amidst the white shafts of light a procession appears. A man clothed in black rests the weight of a coffin on his shoulder. It is the Guardian of the Cause and he bears the mortal remains of the Purest Branch, Bahá'u'lláh's beloved son. Slowly he and his fellow bearers mount the narrow path and in silence approach the house adjacent to the resting place of the Greatest Holy Leaf. A devoted servant speeds ahead with rug and candelabra from the Holy Shrines and swiftly prepares the room. The gentle, strong face of the Guardian appears as he enters the door, that precious weight always on his shoulder, and the coffin is laid temporarily to rest in a humble room, facing Bahjí, the Qiblih of the Faith. Again those devoted servants, led by their Guardian, return to the gate and again remount the path with another sacred burden, this time the body of the wife of Bahá'u'lláh, the mother of the Master.

What a wave of joy seems to come onward with those simple processions! A joy indefinable, touched with deep tenderness and pathos. Like a great white pearl the marble temple marking the grave of Bahíyyih Khánum glows in the light of its reflectors, seeming afire on the dark mountain side, lighting up and watching over those two approaching the scene of their last resting place.

When we enter to pay our respects to those beloved, revered and long since departed ones, their presence seems to fill the room. At last, after seventy years, that saintly mother lies reunited beside her son of whom Bahá'u'lláh wrote: 'He was created of the light of Bahá.' Side by side, facing 'Akká, the sweet fumes of attar of rose with which they have been anointed by the Guardian filling the room, they lie. And above them, lit by the flickering lights of the sentinel candles, the picture of The Greatest Holy Leaf hangs, her beautiful eyes, so full of love and that purity which is goodness itself, looking out over her mother and brother. What cause for joy and gratitude!

That tender youth, born to affliction, reared in exile, died in prison, buried in solitary haste! Here he lies,

THE BURIAL OF THE PUREST BRANCH

raised up from the earth by the hands of the Guardian of his Father's Faith, removed from the lonely isolation of the Arab cemetery where he had been interred so long ago and placed beside his illustrious sister and holy mother, that mother who was affectionately known as 'Búyúk Khánum' or 'Great Lady'. Slender, stately, lovely to look on with white skin and blue eyes and dark hair; she who, when Bahá'u'lláh was thrown into the dungeon of Ṭihrán, was abandoned by friend and foe alike and who purchased food for her children by selling the gold buttons of her robes; she who was forced to leave this same son, then a delicate child of four, behind her when she followed Bahá'u'lláh into exile; she whose tender hands, unaccustomed to work, bled as she washed the clothes of her family; who remained patient, devout, serene and selfless to the end of her life, and who was laid to rest near 'Akká in a cemetery away from her son, now lies beside him, so to remain forever more.

As we meditate beside those two eloquent coffins, covered with woven cloths, strewn with jasmine from the Threshold of the Báb's Tomb, so all pervading is the presence of their spirits – or maybe it is their memory, as perfume lingers when the flower is withered – that the very room they rest in for so short a while becomes itself filled with the sweet peace of a shrine.

Not only has the Guardian raised them to rest in their rightful graves, put them where the whole world may see their honour and their glory, but in some mysterious way he has given them back to us. So long ago they passed away, so quietly, in days of such turmoil and oppression, were they laid to rest, that their places, at least to us of the West, were on written pages of the history of our Faith. But now their places are in our hearts. The veil of time and obscurity separating us has been rent asunder, and we find, to our joy and astonishment, two glowing and holy figures drawing nigh to us, entering into our lives, and ready to help us on that path which leads to their Lord and ours, Bahá'u'lláh.

How warm and living his personality suddenly seems, no longer a name, albeit a revered one, Mihdí, the Purest Branch, but a sweet and selfless youth filled with love and devotion for Him who was not only his earthly but heavenly Father as well. Slight of frame, small of stature, black of hair, scarce twenty years of age, when at the time of his death he acted as the amanuensis of Bahá'u'lláh and the character of his script has remained to us as a tender reminder that he stood only on the threshold of manhood.

Bahá'u'lláh Himself in numerous Tablets has mentioned this beloved son of His, recounting His long separation from him when he was left behind in Írán and was deprived of his family; how later he suffered the exiles and imprisonments of his Father until that fateful day when, as Bahá'u'lláh wrote: 'He has suffered martyrdom at a time when he lay imprisoned at the hands of his enemies.'

The cruelty of exile and banishment became the rigour of complete incarceration during Mihdí's short life time. Upon entering the prison city of 'Akká they were confined in the barracks itself, and it was during this strict period of Bahá'u'lláh's imprisonment, when they suffered the greatest privations and were the victims of terrible epidemics, that the Purest Branch passed away. No one of the devout and faithful, who, some on foot, some on mule back, made the long and arduous journey to see the face of their Lord, was admitted to His presence. They were forced to content themselves with a brief glimpse of Him as He stood in a window facing the little hill beyond the walls and moat where they were wont to await His appearance.

It was under such circumstances that one night, whilst walking on the roof of the fortress, the Purest Branch fell through the opening leading below and was fatally injured. It was the custom of those prisoners to get what air and exercise they could in this manner, and no doubt that youth, lost to all but his thoughts and meditations, stepped unawares through the unguarded sky light. Although the ceilings of oriental rooms are very high, it was not a fall which necessarily would cause the death of a person. But the Purest Branch was terribly injured. He bled profusely from the mouth, and his thigh was so battered and bleeding that his garment could not be removed but was torn from him – that pitiful relic which the Greatest Holy Leaf preserved for posterity and which to this day may be seen with the stains of his life's blood upon it. He survived for about thirty hours after the fall. The doctors, hastily called in, were powerless to help him, but we cannot but believe that it lay within the power of his Father to spare his life, if He had so willed it.

Bahá'u'lláh asked of His dying son if he desired to live, but he replied that his sole desire was that the gates of the prison should be opened so that the believers might visit their Lord. Bahá'u'lláh granted that youth's earnest wish and sat beside His youngest son as they made him ready for the grave, and it was in those tragic circumstances that He revealed the following: 'At this very moment My son is being washed before My face after Our having sacrificed him in the Most Great Prison . . .' 'Glorified art Thou, O Lord, My God! Thou seest Me in the hands of Mine enemies, and My son blood-stained before My face!' Such sentences as these were wrung from the heart of the Blessed Beauty as He gazed upon His child. But then thundering forth came these marvellous words: 'I have, O My Lord, offered up that which Thou has given Me, that Thy servants may be quickened and all that dwell on earth be united.' The tremendous significance of these words is inescapable; Bahá'u'lláh designates to His own child the *rôle* of blood offering in order that the unity of all men which He has proclaimed may come about. The sacrifice of Isaac by Abraham is accomplished.

After, in secrecy, poverty, and haste, the Purest Branch had been interred, his gentle mother, the victim of so many sorrows and deprivations, saddened and wept unceasingly. Bahá'u'lláh on learning of her plight came to her and assured her she had no cause for grief for God had accepted this precious son as His Ransom to draw not only the believers nigh unto their Lord but to unify all the sons of men. After hearing these words that saintly soul was greatly comforted and ceased to mourn her heavy loss.

And who was such a mother? Not merely a holy and faithful woman, willing in the path of God to sacrifice her all, but she of whom Isaiah, in his 54th chapter, says: 'For thy Maker is thy husband; the LORD of hosts is his name; and thy Redeemer the Holy One of Israel; the God of the whole earth shall he be called.' 'For the mountains shall depart, and the hills be removed; but my kindness shall not depart from thee, neither shall the covenant of my peace be removed, saith the LORD that hath mercy on thee.' And she to whom Bahá'u'lláh revealed the following: 'Hear thou Me once again, God is well pleased with thee . . . He hath made thee to be His companion in every one of His worlds and hath nourished thee with His meeting and presence so long as His name and His remembrance and His kingdom and His empire shall endure.'

How fleeting and priceless the days that this mother and son lie side by side in that small room! To be privileged to draw close – in that strange and pitiful closeness one feels to a coffin in which all that remains of dear ones after the soul has flown rests, a token and reminder of our common mortality and immortality – is something never to be forgotten. Thousands will read these Prayers and Tablets of Bahá'u'lláh and 'Abdu'l-Bahá forever immortalizing them. They will supplicate those radiant spirits to intercede on their behalf. They will seek humbly to follow in their noble footsteps. But it will never, so it seems to me, be as sweet and touching as to see them lying there together under the watchful eyes of Bahíyyih Khánum.

Whilst their tombs were still in process of excavation from the solid rock of the mountain, the Guardian had learned that the Covenant-Breakers were protesting against the right of the Bahá'ís to remove the Mother and brother of 'Abdu'l-Bahá to new graves, actually having the temerity to represent to the government their so called claim as relatives of the deceased. As soon, however, as the civil authorities had the true state of facts made clear to them – that these same relatives had been the arch-enemies of the Master and His family, had left the true Cause of Bahá'u'lláh to follow their own devices, and had been denounced by 'Abdu'l-Bahá in His Will and Testament – they approved the plan of the Guardian and immediately issued the necessary papers for the exhumation of the bodies. Without risking further delay Shoghi Effendi, two days later, himself removed the Purest Branch and his mother to Mount Carmel where, watched over by the loving devotion of the believers, and safeguarded from any danger of insult or injury, they could await, close to Bahíyyih Khánum's shrine, their reinterment.

The last stone is laid in the two vaults, the floors are paved in marble, the name plates fixed to mark their heads, the earth smoothed out, the path that leads to their last resting place built, but storm and rain sweep unceasingly over the crest of the mountain postponing the final arrangements until the day before Christmas dawns, bright and clear, as if a sign that this is the appointed time. At sunset we all gather in that humble, twice blessed house. We hear the voice of one of the oldest and most devoted believers of the Near East raised, at the command of his Guardian, in prayer. Tremulous, faint, yet filled with a poignant faith and love hard to describe but never to be forgotten, he prays. As voice follows voice, one of them, that of the Guardian himself, it seems as if one could almost hear the refrain of those prayers sung in triumphant joy by an invisible concourse on high.

And now, again on the shoulder of the Guardian, they are borne forth to lie in state in the Holy Tomb of the Báb. Side by side, far greater than the great of this world, they lie by that sacred threshold, facing

Bahjí, with candles burning at their heads and flowers before their feet. It is the eve of the birth of Christ. She who was foretold of Isaiah, he who was the son of Him of Whom Jesus said: 'Howbeit when he, the Spirit of truth, is come, he will guide you into all truth,' rest quietly here their last night before the earth hides them forever more from the eyes of men.

The following sunset we gather once again in that Holy Shrine. The Guardian chants the Tablet of Visitation, first in the Tomb of the Báb, then in the Tomb of the Master. The privileged friends who have been able to make the pilgrimage to Haifa for this sacred occasion enter with the Guardian a second time the Báb's Shrine. Slowly, held aloft on the hands of the faithful, led by Shoghi Effendi, who never relinquishes his precious burden, first the mother of 'Abdu'l-Bahá and then the Purest Branch are ushered from that Holy Spot. Once they circumambulate the Shrines, the coffin of beloved Mihdí, supported by the Guardian, followed by that of the Master's mother, passes us slowly by. Around the Shrine, onward through the lighted garden, down the white path, out onto the moonlit road, that solemn procession passes. High, seeming to move of themselves, above the heads of those following, the coffins wend their way. They mount the steps and once again enter that gate leading to Bahíyyih Khánum's resting place. They pass before us, outlined against the night sky, across whose face fitful clouds make sport of the full moon. They approach, the face of the Guardian close to that priceless burden he bears. They pass on towards the waiting vaults.

Now they lay the Purest Branch to rest. Shoghi Effendi himself enters the carpeted vault and gently eases the coffin to its preordained place. He himself strews it with flowers, his hands the last to caress it. The mother of the Master is then placed in the same manner by the Guardian in the neighbouring vault. Not six feet apart they rest. The silent faces of the believers in the brilliant light of the lamps, form a waiting circle. Masons are called to seal the tombs. Respectfully and deftly they fulfil their task. Flowers are heaped upon the vaults and the Guardian sprinkles a vial of attar of rose upon them. The pungent scent is caught up on the breeze and bathes our faces. And now the voice of Shoghi Effendi is raised as he chants those tablets revealed by Bahá'u'lláh and destined by Him to be read at their graves.

Surely this is a dream? It cannot be I that stand here gazing at these new-made graves, laid in the breast of ancient Carmel! Beneath me stretches an endless vista. 'Akká gleams white across the bay, that onetime prison city where these two were so long captives, near which they were once buried. The reaches of the sea and plain lie before me, opening out to where the moon silvers the rims of the mountains of the Holy Land, the Land of the Prophets, the Land of the loved ones of God, the

Land chosen to be the Seat of the Ark of God in this most glorious Day. Forever and increasingly about the resting place of this mother, sister, brother of 'Abdu'l-Bahá, the life-giving activities of their Faith will gather. Close to them, focused on their shrines, great institutions will rise to strengthen the soul and body of mankind. And forever interwoven with those institutions will be the memory and example of these three holy persons. Their way has become our way and they lead us on before, heading the ranks of Bahá'u'lláh's followers.

Bibliography

'Abdu'l-Bahá. *Memorials of the Faithful.* Wilmette, IL: Bahá'í Publishing Trust, 1991.
— *The Promulgation of Universal Peace.* Wilmette, IL: Bahá'í Publishing Trust, 1982.
— *Selections from the Writings of 'Abdu'l-Bahá.* Haifa: Bahá'í World Centre, 1978.
— *Some Answered Questions.* Haifa: Bahá'í World Centre, 2014.
— *The Will and Testament of 'Abdu'l-Bahá.* Wilmette, IL: Bahá'í Publishing Trust, 1991.

Abdul Baha on Divine Philosophy. Boston: The Tudor Press, 1918.

The Báb. *Selections from the Writings of the Báb.* Haifa: Bahá'í World Centre, 1976.

Badiei, Amir. *Stories told by 'Abdu'l-Bahá.* Oxford: George Ronald, 2003.

Bagdadi, Zia. "Abdu'l-Bahá in America". *Star of the West,* vol. 19, no. 5 (Aug. 1928), p. 141.

Bahá'í International Community. *Valuing Spirituality in Development: Initial Considerations Regarding the Creation of Spiritually Based Indicators for Development.* London: Bahá'í Publishing Trust, 1998. A concept paper presented to the 'World Faiths and Development Dialogue' hosted by the President of the World Bank and the Archbishop of Canterbury at Lambeth Palace, London, 18–19 February 1998. https://www.bic.org/statements/valuing-spirituality-development#Om7hJV24DLwEuJPZ.97

The Bahá'í World, vols. 1–12, 1925–54. rpt. Wilmette, IL: Bahá'í Publishing Trust, 1980.

The Bahá'í World. vol. 15. Haifa: Bahá'í World Centre, 1976.

Bahá'u'lláh. *Epistle to the Son of the Wolf*. Wilmette, IL: Bahá'í Publishing Trust, 1988.
— *Gleanings from the Writings of Bahá'u'lláh*. Wilmette, IL: Bahá'í Publishing Trust, 1990.
— *Kitáb-i-Íqán*. Wilmette, IL: Bahá'í Publishing Trust, 1989.
— *Prayers and Meditations*. Wilmette, IL: Bahá'í Publishing Trust, 1987.
— *The Summons of the Lord of Hosts: Tablets of Bahá'u'lláh*. Haifa: Bahá'í World Centre, 2002.
— *Tablets of Bahá'u'lláh*. Wilmette, IL: Bahá'í Publishing Trust, 1988.

Bahíyyih Khánum, the Greatest Holy Leaf: A Compilation from Bahá'í Sacred Texts and Writings of the Guardian of the Faith and Bahíyyih Khánum's Own Letters. Haifa: Bahá'í World Centre, 1982.

Baker, Effie. Letter addressed to the Bahá'ís of Melbourne, Adelaide, Perth, Tasmania and Sydney, 29 March 1925.

Balyuzi, H.M. *Bahá'u'lláh: The King of Glory*. Oxford: George Ronald, 1980.

Barnes, Kiser D. *Mírzá Mihdí's Five Smooth Stones*. Johannesburg: Bahá'í Publishing Trust, 2005.

Beveridge, Kent. 'From Adrianople to 'Akká: The Austrian Lloyd'. http://hurqalya.ucmerced.edu/sites/hurqalya.ucmerced.edu/files/page/documents/beveridge.pdf

The Bible
  KJV: Kings James Version
  Douay-Rheims
  NCV: New Century Version
  NIRV: New International Readers Version
  NIV: New International Version
  NKJV: New Kings James Version
  RSV: Revised Standard Version

Blomfield, Lady [Sitárih Khánum; Sara Louise]. *The Chosen Highway*. Oxford: George Ronald, rpt. 2007.

Bonapart, Napoleon (Emperor of the French 1769 – Napoleon

I). A selection from the letters and despatches of the first Napoleon. Reproduction. Charleston, NC: Nabu Press 2010.

Brown, Ramona Allen. *Memories of 'Abdu'l-Bahá*. Wilmette, IL: Bahá'í Publishing Trust, 1980.

Browne, Edward G. 'Introduction', ['Abdu'l-Bahá], *A Traveller's Narrative Written to Illustrate the Episode of the Báb* (trans. E.G. Browne). 2 vols. Cambridge: Cambridge University Press, 1891.

— *Materials for the Study of the Babi Religion*. Cambridge: Cambridge University Press, 1918.

'Commemoration at the World Centre', *Bahá'í World*, vol. 15, p. 163.

Crown of Glory: Memoirs of Jináb-i-Azíz'u'lláh Azízí. Iran: Bahá'í Publishing Trust, 1976. (Translated from the original Persian by Christopher and Nahzy Buck. English translation edited by Hamid and Sandra Azizi, 1991. Available online at: http://bahai-library.com/pdf/a/azizi_crown_glory.pdf

Der Matossian, Bedross. *Shattered Dreams of Revolution: From Liberty to Violence in the Late Ottoman Empire*. Palo Alto, CA: Stanford University Press, 2014.

'Diary of Mirza Ahmad Sohrab', 5 July 1914; in 'Life in the Most Great Prison', *Star of the West*, vol. 8, no. 13 (4 Nov. 1917), p. 173.

'Diary of Mirza Sohrab', 30 April 1914, in *Star of the West*, vol. 8, no. 13, (4 Nov 1917), pp. 169–70.

The Divine Art of Living: Selections from the Writings of Bahá'u'lláh and 'Abdu'l-Bahá. Compiled by Mabel Hyde Paine, revised by Anne Marie Scheffer. Wilmette, IL: Bahá'í Publishing Trust, 1986.

Fadil, Asadu'llah. 'The Life of Baha'u'llah', part II, *Star of the West*, vol. 14, no. 11, p. 328.

Jinab-i-Fadil. 'The Glory of Deeds', in *Star of the West*, vol. 14, no. 6, p. 174. Available online at: https://bahai.works/Star_of_the_West/Volume_14/Issue_6#pg174]

Faizi, Abu'l-Qasim. (1968). 'From Adrianople to 'Akká', in Shirley Macias, *The Conqueror of Hearts*. Unpublished MS in the Afnan Library, Sandy, Bedfordshire, UK, and published online at http://bahai-library.com/faizi_adrianople_akka

Handal, Boris. *El Concurso en Lo Alto*. Lima: Propaceb, 1985.

'Holy place restored and open to pilgrims', Bahá'í World News Service, 24 November 2004. http://news.bahai.org/story/336

Honnold, Annamarie. *Vignettes from the Life of 'Abdu'l-Bahá*. Oxford: George Ronald, rev. ed. 1991.

Ives, Howard Colby. *Portals to Freedom*. London: George Ronald, 1967.

Khadem, Zikrullah. 'The Purest Branch and the New Order', in *Payám-i-Bahá'í*, vol. 79. no. 11 (June 1986).

Khan, Janet A. *Prophet's Daughter: The Life and Legacy of Bahíyyih Khánum, Outstanding Heroine of the Bahá'í Faith*. Wilmette, IL: Bahá'í Publishing Trust, 2005.

Latimer, George Orr. *The Light of the World*. Haifa, Palestine: n.p., 1920.

'Life in the Most Great Prison', in 'The Hundredth Anniversary of the Birth of Baha'o'llah', *Star of the West*, vol. 8, no. 13, p. 171.

Ma'ani, Baharieh Rouhani. *Leaves of the Twin Divine Trees*. Oxford: George Ronald, 2008.

McLean, J.A. 'Divine Simplicity: Remembering the last Hand of the Cause of God 'Ali-Muhammad Varqá'. http://bahai-library.com/mclean_divine_simplicity

Momen, Moojan. *The Bábí and Bahá'í Religions, 1844–1944. Some Contemporary Western Accounts*. Oxford: George Ronald, 1981.

— 'The Bahá'í Community of Iran: Patterns of Exile and Problems of Communication', in Asghar Fathi, ed. *Iranian Refugees and Exiles Since Khomeini*. Costa Mesa. CA: Mazda Publishers, 1991, pp. 21–36.

— 'Cyprus Exiles', *Bahá'í Studies Bulletin*, vol. 5, no. 3 – vol. 6, no. 1 (June 1991), pp. 84–113. Also available at: http:/www.momen.org/relstud/CyprusEx.htm

'Music: Its Material and Spiritual Significance', *Star of the West*, vol. 15, no. 5 (Aug. 1924), p. 130.

Nabíl-i-A'ẓam. *The Dawn-Breakers: Nabíl's Narrative of the Early Days of the Bahá'í Revelation*. Wilmette, IL: Bahá'í Publishing Trust, 1970.

Neugeboren, Jay. *An Orphan's Tale*. Ann Arbor, MI: Dzanc Books, 1976.

The Oxford English Dictionary, vol. 6. Oxford: Clarendon Press, 1970.

Paine, Mabel Hyde. Unpublished Memoirs.

Phelps, Myron H. *Abbas Effendi: His Life and Teachings*. New York: G. P. Putnam's Son, 1903.

Philipp, Thomas. 'The Rise and Fall of Acre: Population and Economy between 1700 and 1850'. *Revue du Monde Musulman et de la Méditerranée*, vol. 55–6 (1990), 124–40.

Rabbani, Rúḥíyyih. 'The Burial of the Purest Branch and the Mother of 'Abdu'l-Bahá', in *Bahá'í World*, vol. 8, pp. 253–8.
— *A Manual for Pioneers*. New Delhi: Bahá'í Publishing Trust, 1974.
— *The Priceless Pearl*. London: Bahá'í Publishing Trust, 1969.

Renshaw, Amy. *Voyage of Love: 'Abdu'l-Bahá in North America*. Wilmette, IL: Bellwood Press, 2010.

Rosenberg, E. J. [Ethel Jenner]. Account of 'Zea Khanom', Notes of Miss E.J. Rosenberg, Haifa, February and March 1901, in 'Life in the Most Great Prison', *Star of the West*, vol. 8, no. 13 (4 Nov. 1917), p. 172.

Ruhe, David S. *Door of Hope*. Oxford: George Ronald, 2nd rev. ed., 2001.
— *Robe of Light: The Persian Years of the Supreme Prophet Bahá'u'lláh, 1817–1853*. Oxford: George Ronald, 1994.

Salmání, Ustád Muhammad-'Alíy-i. *My Memories of Bahá'u'lláh*. Los Angeles: Kalimát Press, 1982.

Shoghi Effendi. *The Advent of Divine Justice*. Wilmette, IL: Bahá'í Publishing Trust, 1990.
— *God Passes By*. Wilmette, IL: Bahá'í Publishing Trust, rev. ed. 1995.
— *Messages to America*. Wilmette, IL: Bahá'í Publishing Committee, 1947.
— *The Promised Day is Come*. Wilmette, IL: Bahá'í Publishing Trust, rev. ed. 1980.
— *This Decisive Hour: Messages from Shoghi Effendi to the North American Bahá'ís, 1932–1946*. Wilmette, IL: Bahá'í Publishing Trust, 2002.
— *The Unfolding Destiny of the British Bahá'í Community: The Messages of the Guardian of the Bahá'í Faith to the Bahá'ís of the British Isles*. London: Bahá'í Publishing Trust, 1981.

Star of the West. rpt. Oxford: George Ronald, 1984.

'Statistics', Bahá'í World News Service. http://news.bahai.org/media-information/statistics

Taherzadeh, Adib. *The Child of the Covenant*. Oxford, George Ronald, 2000.
— *The Revelation of Bahá'u'lláh*, vol. 1. Oxford: George Ronald, 1974.
— *The Revelation of Bahá'u'lláh*, vol. 2. Oxford: George Ronald, 1977.
— *The Revelation of Bahá'u'lláh*, vol. 3. Oxford: George Ronald, 1983.
— 'Three Momentous Years of the Heroic Age: 1868–1870', in *Bahá'í World*, vol. 15, p. 771.

The Universal House of Justice. Letter to All National Spiritual Assemblies, 25 March 1970.
— Letter to Bahá'í Youth in Every Land, 10 June 1966.
— Message to the First Oceanic Conference, Palermo, Sicily, August 1968.

Notes and References

Frontispiece
1. Bahá'u'lláh, *Prayers and Meditations*, p. 34.
2. Bahá'u'lláh, quoted in a letter of Shoghi Effendi, 21 December 1939, in *This Decisive Hour*, p. 46.

Foreword
1. Shoghi Effendi, *God Passes By*, p. 409.
2. ibid. p. 410.
3. ibid. pp. 403–10.
4. ibid. p. 188.
5. Bahá'u'lláh, *Summons of the Lord of Hosts*, p. 144.
6. Bahá'u'lláh, quoted in Shoghi Effendi, *God Passes By*, p. 188

1 'Akká, the Most Great Prison
1. Judges 1:31 KJV.
2. Hosea 2:15; Isaiah 65:10; Joshua 7:24, 26; 15:7 KJV.
3. Bahá'u'lláh, *Epistle to the Son of the Wolf*, p. 179.
4. Bonaparte, *Selection from the letters and despatches*, p. 252.
5. Der Matossian, *Shattered Dreams*, p. 170.
6. Psalms 60:9; 108:10 KJV.
7. Hosea 2:15 KJV.
8. Psalms 24:7–10 KJV.
9. Hosea 2:15 NIV.
10. Psalms 31:21 Douay-Rheims Bible.
11. Psalms 60:9; 108:10 NIV.
12. Psalms 24:7–10 NIV.
13. Ezekiel 43:1–2, 4 NIV.
14. Amos 1:2 NCV.
15. Micah 7:12 KJV.
16. 'Abdu'l-Bahá, *Some Answered Questions*, p. 32.
17. Bahá'u'lláh, *Gleanings*, p. 345.
18. Bahá'u'lláh, quoted in Shoghi Effendi, *God Passes By*, p. 186.
19. ibid. pp. 185–6.
20. Handal, *El Concurso en Lo Alto*.

21. Shoghi Effendi, *God Passes By*, p. 193.
22. See Blomfield, *Chosen Highway*, p. 64.
23. ibid. p. 185.

2 The Purest Branch

1. Barnes, *Mírzá Mihdí's Five Smooth Stones*, p. 36.
2. A follower of the Báb, 1819–50, Bahá'u'lláh's Prophet-Herald.
3. Blomfield, *Chosen Highway*, p. 45. Mírzá Mihdí was about four years old in 1853.
4. ibid.
5. Khadem, 'The Purest Branch and the New Order', p. 11.
6. Ruhe, *Robe of Light*, p. 165.
7. Balyuzi, *King of Glory*, p. 102.
8. Matthew 18:3 NIV.
9. Bahá'u'lláh, *Kitáb-i-Íqán*, p. 22.
10. Shoghi Effendi, *God Passes By*, p. 102.
11. Salmání, *My Memories of Bahá'u'lláh*, p. 34.
12. Fadil, 'The Life of Baha'u'llah', part II, *Star of the West*, vol. 14, no. 11, p. 328.
13. Balyuzi, *King of Glory*, p. 314.
14. Ḥusayn-i-Áshchí, quoted in Taherzadeh, *Revelation of Bahá'u'lláh*, vol. 3, p. 206.
15. Bahá'u'lláh, quoted in Shoghi Effendi, *God Passes By*, p. 187.

3 Early Years in Tehran

1. Shoghi Effendi, *God Passes By*, p. 108.
2. Rabbaní, Rúḥíyyih Khánum, in 'The Burial of the Purest Branch and the Mother of 'Abdu'l-Bahá, in *Bahá'í World*, vol. 8, p. 255.
3. Balyuzi, *King of Glory*, p. 23.
4. Ásíyih is identified in Islamic Traditions as the wife of Pharaoh. 'Abdu'l-Bahá identifies her as the daughter of Pharaoh ('Abdu'l-Bahá, *Promulgation*, p. 175).
5. Blomfield, *Chosen Highway*, p. 39.
6. ibid. pp. 39–40.
7. The journey lasted three months, from 12 January to 8 April 1853.
8. Blomfield, *Chosen Highway*, pp. 40–6. Emphasis in the original.

4 Exile in Baghdad, Constantinople and Adrianople

1. Blomfield, *Chosen Highway*, pp. 46–7.
2. Shoghi Effendi, *God Passes By*, pp. 129–30.
3. Bahá'u'lláh, *Gleanings*, pp. 111–14.
4. Attributed to 'Abdu'l-Bahá, in Rabbani, *Manual for Pioneers*, p. 20.
5. Attributed to 'Abdu'l-Bahá, in the 'Diary of Mirza Sohrab', 30 April 1914, in *Star of the West*, vol. 8, no. 13, pp. 169–70.
6. Bahá'u'lláh, *Gleanings*, pp. 126–7.
7. Bahá'u'lláh, quoted in Shoghi Effendi, *God Passes By*, p. 161.
8. Browne, Introduction to *Traveller's Narrative*, pp. xxxix–xl.
9. Mírzá Haydar-'Alí, quoted in Taherzadeh, *Revelation of Bahá'u'lláh*, vol. 2, p. 195.
10. Shoghi Effendi, *God Passes By*, p. 165.
11. Mírzá Mihdí, quoted in Salmání, *My Memories of Bahá'u'lláh*, p. 34.
12. See Taherzadeh, *Revelation of Bahá'u'lláh*, vol. 2, p. 401.
13. See Taherzadeh, *Child of the Covenant*, p. 89.
14. Bahá'u'lláh, quoted in Shoghi Effendi, *God Passes By*, p. 184.

5 The Long Journey to 'Akká

1. Quoted in Phelps, *Life and Teachings of Abbas Effendi*, pp. 47–53.
2. Shoghi Effendi, *God Passes By*, p. 182.
3. Faizi, 'From Adrianople to 'Akká', p. 14.
4. Momen, *Bábí and Bahá'í Religions*, p. 205.
5. Quoted in Balyuzi, *King of Glory*, p. 264.
6. Blomfield, *Chosen Highway*, p. 65.
7. Beveridge, 'From Adrianople to 'Akká: The Austrian Lloyd'. http://hurqalya.ucmerced.edu/sites/hurqalya.ucmerced.edu/files/page/documents/beveridge.pdf. Accessed 22 May 2016.
8. Balyuzi, *King of Glory*, pp. 277–9.
9. Momen, 'Cyprus Exiles', *Bahá'í Studies Bulletin*, vol. 5, no. 3 – vol. 6, no. 1, pp. 84–113. Also available at: http:/www.momen.org/relstud/CyprusEx.htm
10. Faizi, 'From Adrianople to 'Akká', p. 15.
11. Balyuzi, *King of Glory*, p. 264.
12. 'Abdu'l-Bahá, *Memorials of the Faithful*, pp. 146–7.
13. Quoted in Blomfield, *Chosen Highway*, p. 65.

14. Quoted in Phelps, *Life and Teachings of Abbas Effendi*, pp. 53–4.
15. Balyuzi, *King of Glory*, p. 267.
16. ibid.
17. From the unpublished history of Nabíl, quoted in Balyuzi, *King of Glory*, p. 268.
18. Blomfield, *Chosen Highway*, p. 65.
19. ibid.
20. ibid. p. 66.
21. Quoted in Phelps, *Life and Teachings of Abbas Effendi*, p. 55.
22. The Universal House of Justice, Message to the First Oceanic Conference, Palermo, Sicily, August 1968.

6 The Disembarkation in 'Akká

1. Ruhe, *Door of Hope*, p. 22.
2. Shoghi Effendi, *God Passes By*, p. 182.
3. Quoted in Blomfield, *Chosen Highway*, p. 66.
4. Attributed to 'Abdu'l-Bahá, in 'Life in the Most Great Prison', in 'The Hundredth Anniversary of the Birth of Baha'o'llah', *Star of the West*, vol. 8, no. 13, p. 171.
5. Phelps, *Life and Teachings of Abbas Effendi*, p. 56.
6. Bahíyyih Khánum quoted in ibid. p. 56.
7. Quoted in Faizi, 'From Adrianople to 'Akká'.
8. Quoted in Paine, Unpublished Memoirs, pp. 37–8.
9. Philipp, 'Rise and Fall of Acre', *Revue du Monde Musulman et de la Méditerranée*, vol. 55, pp. 124–40.
10. Attributed to 'Abdu'l-Bahá, in 'Life in the Most Great Prison', in 'The Hundredth Anniversary of the Birth of Baha'o'llah', *Star of the West*, vol. 8, no. 13, p. 171.
11. Phelps, *Life and Teachings of Abbas Effendi*, pp. 56–7.
12. Latimer, *Light of the World*, pp. 132–3.
13. Attributed to 'Abdu'l-Bahá in the diary of Dr Ḥabíb Mu'ayyad, cited in Ruhe, *Door of Hope*, p. 221.
14. Taherzadeh, *Revelation of Bahá'u'lláh*, vol. 3, pp. 12–13.
15. Blomfield, *Chosen Highway*, p. 240.
16. The Báb.
17. Quoted in Shoghi Effendi, *God Passes By*, p. 184.
18. Bahá'u'lláh, quoted in ibid. p. 185.
19. Faizi, 'From Adrianople to 'Akká', pp. 24–5.
20. Phelps, *Life and Teachings of Abbas Effendi*, pp. 58–9.
21. Ezekiel 43:2 NIRV.

22. Psalms 60:9 RSV.
23. Ezekiel 43:1 RSV.
24. Hosea 2:15 RSV.
25. Psalms 132:14 NKJV.

7 Life in the Barracks

1. See Taherzadeh, *Revelation of Bahá'u'lláh*, vol. 3, p. 19.
2. Quoted in Phelps, *Life and Teachings of Abbas Effendi*, pp. 57–8.
3. Quoted in Latimer, *Light of the World*.
4. Quoted in Shoghi Effendi, *God Passes By*, p. 187.
5. Taherzadeh, *Revelation of Bahá'u'lláh*, vol. 3, p. 17.
6. *Abdul Baha on Divine Philosophy*, p. 18.
7. Quoted in Balyuzi, *King of Glory*, p. 276.
8. 'Abdu'l-Bahá, in 'Life in the Most Great Prison', *Star of the West*, vol. 8, no. 13 (4 Nov. 1917), p. 172.
9. 'Abdu'l-Bahá, *Memorials of the Faithful*, p. 20.
10. Bahá'í International Community, 'Holy place restored and open to pilgrims', Bahá'í World News Service, November 2004. http://news.bahai.org/story/336
11. Bahá'u'lláh, 'Lawḥ-i-Ra'ís', *Summons of the Lord of Hosts*, para. 27, p. 172.
12. 'Abdu'l-Bahá, *Memorials of the Faithful*, p. 171.
13. Quoted in Balyuzi, *King of Glory*, p. 109.
14. Paine, Unpublished Memoirs. p. 38.
15. 'Abdu'l-Bahá, *Memorials of the Faithful*, p. 163.
16. ibid. pp. 163–4.
17. Taherzadeh, *Revelation of Bahá'u'lláh*, vol. 3, p. 72.
18. Balyuzi, *King of Glory*, p. 287.
19. Phelps, *Life and Teachings of Abbas Effendi*, pp. 5–7.
20. Bahíyyih Khánum, quoted in 'Diary of Mirza Ahmad Sohrab', 5 July 1914; in 'Life in the Most Great Prison', *Star of the West*, vol. 8, no. 13 (4 Nov. 1917), p. 173.
21. Quoted in Phelps, *Life and Teachings of Abbas Effendi*, p. 66.
22. 'Abdu'l-Bahá, in Zia Bagdadi, "'Abdu'l-Bahá in America', *Star of the West*, vol. 19, no. 5 (Aug. 1928), p. 141.
23. 'Abdu'l-Bahá, quoted from the Notes of Miss E.J. Rosenberg, Haifa, February, March 1901; in 'Life in the Most Great Prison', *Star of the West*, vol. 8, no. 13 (4 Nov. 1917), p. 172.
24. 'Abdu'l-Bahá, in a Tablet to Edward B. Kinney; in 'Music: Its Material and Spiritual Significance', *Star of the West*, vol. 15,

no. 5 (Aug. 1924), p. 130.
25. Taherzadeh, *Revelation of Bahá'u'lláh*, vol. 3, p. 53.
26. Phelps, *Life and Teachings of Abbas Effendi*, pp. 70–1.
27. Taherzadeh, *Revelation of Bahá'u'lláh*, vol. 3, p. 206.
28. 'Abdu'l-Bahá quoted in *'Abdu'l-Bahá on Divine Philosophy*, p. 18.
29. 'Abdu'l-Bahá, *Memorials of the Faithful*, p. 155.
30. Quoted in Blomfield, *Chosen Highway*, p. 93.
31. Taherzadeh, *Revelation of Bahá'u'lláh*, vol. 3, p. 52.
32. 'Abdu'l-Bahá, *Memorials of the Faithful*, p. 16.
33. Handal, *El Concurso en Lo Alto*, p. 223.
34. Quoted in Balyuzi, *King of Glory*, p. 442.
35. Badiei, *Stories told by 'Abdu'l-Bahá*, p. 101.
36. Latimer, *Light of the World*.
37. Ives, *Portals to Freedom*, p. 120.
38. Brown, *Memories of 'Abdu'l-Bahá*, p. 38.
39. Badiei, *Stories told by 'Abdu'l-Bahá*, pp. 102–3.
40. *Divine Art of Living*, p. 65.
41. ibid. pp. 68–9.
42. Bahá'u'lláh, *Gleanings*, pp. 99–100.

8 The First Bahá'í Pilgrims

1. Shoghi Effendi, *God Passes By*, p. 186.
2. 'Abdu'l-Bahá, *Memorials of the Faithful*, p. 73.
3. ibid. p. 27.
4. ibid. p. 157, regarding Mírzá Ja'far-i-Yazdí.
5. ibid. pp. 48–9.
6. ibid. p. 25.
7. Áqá Sidq-'Alí, quoted in ibid. p. 37.
8. *Crown of Glory*, pp. 126–7. http://bahai-library.com/pdf/a/azizi_crown_glory.pdf
9. The Báb, *Selections*, p. 77.
10. Momen, 'Bahá'í Community of Iran', in Fathi, ed. *Iranian Refugees and Exiles Since Khomeini*, pp. 21–36.
11. Phelps, *Life and Teachings of Abbas Effendi*, p. 65.
12. ibid. p. 54.
13. Bahá'u'lláh, quoted in Ruhe, *Door of Hope*, p. 30.
14. 'Abdu'l-Bahá, *Memorials of the Faithful*, p. 34.
15. Quoted in Taherzadeh, 'Three Momentous Years of the Heroic Age: 1868–1870', in *Bahá'í World*, vol. 15, p. 771.

16. Jinab-i-Fadil, 'Glory of Deeds', in *Star of the West*, vol. 14, issue 6, p. 174.
17. Handal, *El Concurso en Lo Alto*.
18. Honnald, *Vignettes*, p. 119.
19. Quoted in Taherzadeh, *Revelation of Bahá'u'lláh*, vol. 3, p. 66.
20. ibid. pp. 66-7. These are not the exact words of Bahá'u'lláh.
21. ibid. p. 67.
22. ibid. pp. 70-2.
23. 'Abdu'l-Bahá, *Memorials of the Faithful*, p. 52.
24. Shoghi Effendi, *God Passes By*, pp. 187-8.
25. 'Abdu'l-Bahá, *Memorials of the Faithful*, p. 31.
26. ibid. p. 165.
27. Quoted in Blomfield, *Chosen Highway*, pp. 125-7.
28. Taherzadeh, *Revelation of Bahá'u'lláh*, vol. 3, pp. 59-61.
29. Quoted in Shoghi Effendi, *Promised Day Has Come*, p. 68.

9 The Treasure of God in the Holy Land

1. Balyuzi, *King of Glory*, p. 271.
2. Quoted in a letter of Effie Baker addressed to the Bahá'ís of Melbourne, Adelaide, Perth, Tasmania and Sydney, 29 March 1925. See also Taherzadeh, *Revelation of Bahá'u'lláh*, vol. 3, p. 205.
3. Quoted in Nabíl, *Dawn-Breakers*, p. 61.
4. Bahá'u'lláh, quoted in Shoghi Effendi, *Advent of Divine Justice*, p. 82.
5. Bahá'u'lláh, quoted in Shoghi Effendi, *God Passes By*, p. 118.
6. Recounted in Ishráq-i-Khávarí, *Ḥaḍrat-i-Ghuṣnu'lláhu'l-Aṭhar*, pp. 9-14, quoted in Ma'ani, *Leaves of the Twin Divine Trees*, p. 110.
7. Phelps, *Life and Teachings of Abbas Effendi*, pp. 66-7.
8. Quoted in Taherzadeh, *Revelation of Bahá'u'lláh*, vol. 3, p. 206.
9. Letter of Effie Baker addressed to the Bahá'ís of Melbourne, Adelaide, Perth, Tasmania and Sydney, 29 March 1925.
10. McLean, 'Divine Simplicity: Remembering the last Hand of the Cause of God 'Ali-Muhammad Varqá'. http://bahai-library.com/mclean_divine_simplicity
11. One source relates that he was found lying unconscious but recovered awareness later on. See Browne, *Materials for the Study of the Babi Religion*.

12. ibid. pp. 206–7.
13. Taherzadeh, *Revelation of Bahá'u'lláh*, vol. 3, p. 207.
14. Recounted in Ishráq-i-Khávarí, *Ḥaḍrat-i-Ghuṣnu'lláhu'l-Aṭhar*, pp. 9–14, quoted in Ma'ani, *Leaves of the Twin Divine Trees*, p. 110.
15. Phelps, *Life and Teachings of Abbas Effendi*, p. 67.
16. Shoghi Effendi, *Messages to America*, p. 34.
17. Quoted in Balyuzi, *King of Glory*, p. 311.
18. Quoted in Phelps, *Life and Teachings of Abbas Effendi*, p. 68.
19. ibid. pp. 67–8.
20. Taherzadeh, *Revelation of Bahá'u'lláh*, vol. 3, p. 209.
21. Ma'ani, *Leaves of the Twin Divine Trees*, pp. 110–11.
22. Account of 'Zea Khanom' from the notes of Ethel Rosenberg, February and March 1901, in 'Life in the Most Great Prison', *Star of the West*, vol. 8, no. 13, p. 172.
23. See Balyuzi, *King of Glory*, p. 313.
24. Shoghi Effendi, *Messages to America*, p. 31.
25. Quoted in ibid. p. 34.
26. ibid.
27. Ruhe, *Door of Hope*, p. 33.
28. Quoted in Phelps, *Life and Teachings of Abbas Effendi*, pp. 69–70.
29. Bahá'u'lláh, *Gleanings*, p. 10.

10 The Great Redemptive Sacrifice of the Purest Branch
1. Quoted in Shoghi Effendi, *Messages to America*, p. 33.
2. Quoted in Shoghi Effendi, *God Passes By*, pp. 188, 348.
3. Quoted in Shoghi Effendi, *Messages to America*, pp. 33–4.
4. Shoghi Effendi, *God Passes By*, p. 188.
5. Taherzadeh, *Revelation of Bahá'u'lláh*, vol. 3, p. 211.
6. Bahá'u'lláh, *Prayers and Meditations*, pp. 35–6.
7. Quoted in Shoghi Effendi, *Messages to America*, p. 34.
8. ibid.
9. From a letter of the Universal House of Justice to all National Spiritual Assemblies, 25 March 1970, quoting Shoghi Effendi, *God Passes By*, p. 348.
10. 'Commemoration at the World Centre', *Bahá'í World*, vol. 15, p. 163.

11 Life without Mírzá Mihdí
1. Quoted in Shoghi Effendi, *Messages to America*, p. 34.

2. 'Abdu'l-Bahá, *Memorials of the Faithful*, p. 53.
3. Account of 'Zea Khanom' from the notes of Ethel Rosenberg, February and March 1901, in 'Life in the Most Great Prison', *Star of the West*, vol. 8, no. 13, pp. 172–3.
4. Bahá'u'lláh, *Prayers and Meditations*, p. 35.
5. Bahá'u'lláh, *Gleanings*, pp. 132–4.
6. Quoted in Blomfield, *Chosen Highway*, pp. 93–4.
7. Shoghi Effendi, *Messages to America*, p. 36.
8. ibid. pp. 35–6.
9. Bahá'u'lláh, quoted in ibid. pp. 34–5.

12 A Monument to the Purest Branch

1. See Appendix.
2. Shoghi Effendi, *This Decisive Hour*, p. 44.
3. Shoghi Effendi, *Unfolding Destiny*, p. 134.
4. Shoghi Effendi, *This Decisive Hour*, p. 44.
5. ibid. p. 49.
6. Shoghi Effendi, *Messages to America*, p. 33.
7. ibid. pp. 31–3.
8. Shoghi Effendi, *God Passes By*, p. 348.
9. *Bahíyyih Khánum, the Greatest Holy Leaf*, p. 61.
10. Shoghi Effendi, *Messages to America*, p. 36.
11. Isaiah 54:13 KJV.
12. Isaiah 54:11 KJV; see Shoghi Effendi, *Messages to America*, pp. 35–6.

13 The Ode of the Dove

1. See Barnes, *Mírzá Mihdí's Five Smooth Stones*.
2. Shoghi Effendi, *God Passes By*, p. 123.
3. Taherzadeh, *Revelation of Bahá'u'lláh*, vol. 1, p. 63.
4. Quoted in Shoghi Effendi, *God Passes By*, p. 118.
5. Brown, *Materials for the Study of the Bábí Religion*, p. 49.
6. Balyuzi, *King of Glory*, p. 311.
7. Taherzadeh, *Revelation of Bahá'u'lláh*, vol. 3, p. 206.
8. Quoted in ibid.
9. Shoghi Effendi, *God Passes By*, p. 188.
10. Latimer, *Light of the World*, p. 89.
11. Letter of Effie Baker to the Baha'is of Melbourne, Adelaide and Perth Assemblies, 29 March 1925.
12. Latimer, *Light of the World*, pp. 89–96.
13. Bahá'u'lláh, *Summons of the Lord of Hosts*, p. 143.

14. Quoted in Blomfield, *Chosen Highway*, pp. 224–5.
15. 'Holy place restored and open to pilgrims', Bahá'í World News Service, 24 November 2004. http://news.bahai.org/story/336

14 Epilogue

1. 'Abdu'l-Bahá, *Will and Testament*, p. 12.
2. John 15:13 KJV.
3. Ma'ani, *Leaves of the Twin Divine Trees*, p. 150.
4. Genesis 22:1–18.
5. Bahá'u'lláh, *Prayers and Meditations*, p. 11.
6. Shoghi Effendi, *God Passes By*, p. 188.
7. Neugeboren, *An Orphan's Tale*.
8. 'Abdu'l-Bahá, *Selections*, pp. 199–200.
9. Quoted in Shoghi Effendi, *Messages to America*, p. 34.
10. See Bahá'í International Community, 'Valuing Spirituality in Development'. https://www.bic.org/statements/valuingspirituality development#Om7hJV24DLwEuJPZ.97.
11. ibid.
12. Quoted in Rabbani, *Priceless Pearl*, p. 74.
13. Phelps, *Life and Teachings of Abbas Effendi*, p. 67.
14. Taherzadeh, *Revelation of Bahá'u'lláh*, vol. 3, p. 210.
15. Bahá'u'lláh, *Gleanings*, p. 287.
16. See Bahá'u'lláh, *Tablets*, pp. 3–5.
17. See 'Statistics', Bahá'í World News Service. http://news.bahai.org/media-information/statistics
18. From a letter of the Universal House of Justice to Bahá'í Youth in Every Land, 10 June 1966.

Appendix The Burial of the Purest Branch and the Mother of 'Abdu'l-Bahá by Rúḥíyyih Rabbani

1. Rabbani, 'The Burial of the Purest Branch and the Mother of 'Abdu'l-Bahá', *Bahá'í World*, vol. 8, pp. 253–8.

Index

This index is alphabetized word for word. Hyphenated names are considered as two separate words. The words 'a', 'an', 'and', 'after', 'for', 'in', 'is' 'of', 'on', 'the', 'to' and 'with' in entries, as well as the connecters '-i-' and 'y-i-', are ignored. Illustrations are in bold.

'Abbás Effendi, *see* 'Abdu'l-Bahá
'Abbúd, House of, ix, 8, **132-3**
'Abdu'l-Ahad, 94-5, 120
'Abdu'l-Azíz, Sulṭán, viii, 3, 6, **36-7**, 42, 43
  deposed, 190
  edicts exiling Bahá'u'lláh, 4, 8, 17, 39-40, 48, 51, 54, 55, 67, 69, 108, 138
'Abdu'l-Bahá, **36-7**
  and administrative order, 180
  in Adrianople, viii, 51-4, **36-7**
  arrival in 'Akká, 69-80, 86, 87, 89
  'Abdu'l-Bahá's description of, 72, 73, 108-9
  and Badí', 122
  on Bahá'u'lláh, 5
  in the barracks, 78, 83, 86, 90-1, 92, 93, 94, 95, 97, 103, 104, 122, 124-5
  burial place of, 181
  called the 'Master', 50
  childhood of, 21, 22
  children of, 169
  on contentment, 39
  death of Mírzá Mihdí, 146, 150-1
  on declaration of Bahá'u'lláh, 40-1
  denounced by Covenant-breakers, 216
  description of 'Akká, 72
  description of Áqá 'Alíy-i-Qazvíní, 131-2
  duties of, 9, 90, 97, 98-9, 102, 104, 204
  on freedom, 109
  in Gallipoli, 54-5, 57-9
  and the governor, 86
  and the Governor of Adrianople, 50-1
  illness of, 90, 94
  journey from Gallipoli, 50-5, 57-68
  on laughter, 107-9
  on life in the barracks, 86, 87, 89, 90-1, 98-9, 106-9
  on life after death, 199-200
  marriage of, 169
  and Mírzá Asadu'lláh Káshání, 134
  on Mírzá Ja'far, 106-7
  and Mírzá Mihdí, 10, 15-16, 109, 115, 146, 150, 195, 196
  the Most Great Branch, 15
  and the Muftí of 'Akká, 127-9
  on Navváb, 171-2
  on passing of Jináb-i-Muníb, 61-2
  prediction of the taking of 'Akká, 191
  on prison conditions, 90-1, 106, 107-9, 114-16, 117
  sends a letter to Nabíl from ship in Alexandria, 65
  on Shaykh Salmán, 104-5
  a soup-maker, 102
  titles of, 15
  unhygienic conditions, 169
  on Ustád Ismá'íl, 130-1
  wife of (Munírih Khánum), 177, 181
  Will and Testament of, 216
  wisdom of, 124-5, 127, 128
'Abdu'l-Ghaffár, 70
'Abdu'lláh Ṭuzih, 76

'Abdu'r-Raḥím, 136-7
Abraham, xv, 68, 143, 157, 187, 198, 215
Abu'l-Ḥasan-i-Ardikání, ix, 119, **132-3**, 135
Abu'l-Qásim, 89, 154
Adrianople (Edirne), viii, 7, 15, **36-7**, 50, 61, 67, 81, 94, 113, 164, 196
  exile in, 33, 43-9
  journey from, to 'Akká, 50-5, 57-68, 190
  photographs taken in, 194
Aghsán (Branch), 194
Aḥmad-i-Jarráh, Colonel, 125
'Akká, viii, ix, xii, xiv, 1-9, 10, **36-7**, **132-3**
  'Abdu'l-Ahad in, 94-5
  arrival and disembarkation at, 67, 69-80, 213
  described by 'Abdu'l-Bahá, 72, 73, 78
  described by Bahíyyih Khánum, 70, 71, 72, 73, 78
  described by Shoghi Effendi, 70
  significance described by the Universal House of Justice, 67-8
  Azalís in, 113-14
  Bahá'í World Centre, 78-9
  Bahá'ís try to enter, 100
  Bahá'u'lláh and family in houses in, 202
  Bahá'u'lláh's arrival, see Bahá'u'lláh, arrival in 'Akká
  barracks, see barracks, 'Akká
  British capture, 188-9
  designated 'the Most Great Prison', 9
  environment of, 6-7
  exile to, 17, 33, 46, 48, 59
  history of, 1-9
  house of Údí Khammár in, 165
  journey from Adrianople to, 50-5, 57-68
  spiritual significance of, 67-8
  life in, 86, 139-41
  pilgrims in, 113-38
  prophecies of Bahá'u'lláh coming to, 2-5, 48, 49, 76-7, 79
  public baths in, 90, 119
  water in, 6-7
Aleppo, 105, 117, 132, 134, 135
Alexander II, Czar, 124
Alexander the Great, 140
Alexandria, 56, 58-9, 62-6, 69
  Nabíl-i-Azam in, 63-5
'Alí-'Askar, 90-1
'Alíy-i-Mírí, Shaykh (Muftí of 'Akká), 127-9
'Alíy-i-Misrí, Ḥájí, 104
'Alí Páshá (Turkish prime minister), 88, 124, 190
'Alíy-i-Qazvíní, Áqá, 131-2, 135
Amos, 3
Anís, Jináb-i-, 58
Arciduca Ferdinando Massimiliano, viii, 59, **36-7**
Asadu'lláh Káshání, Mírzá, 132-5
Ásíyih Khánum, see Navváb
Austrian Lloyd steamships, 57, 58, 59, 62, 69
Azalís, 113-14
Azím-i-Tafrishí, 103

the Báb, 11, 12, 23, 32, 46, 94, 116, 117, 118, 143, 158, 177, 180-2, 194, 198, 204, 211, 217, 218, 228, 230
Bábís, 11, 12, 23-5, 32-3, 35, 46, 94, 102, 116, 194, 228
Badasht, Conference of, 32
Badí', ix, 122-3, **132-3**, 135, 186-7
Baghdad, viii, 7, 13, **36-7**, 164
  Bahá'u'lláh leaves, 11, 40, 132
  Bahá'u'lláh sent to, 14, 34-6
  exile in, 33, 39, 196
    described by 'Abdu'l-Bahá, 39
    described by Bahíyyih Khánum, 33-5
  Mírzá Mihdí brought to, 11, 14, 81
Bahá'í Faith, xiii, 4-5, 19, 57, 64, 77, 99, 117, 120, 122, 158, 178, 179, 181, 187, 198, 202-5, 210, 212, 220
Bahá'í World Commonwealth, 180-1
Bahá'u'lláh, viii, ix, xi, 32-3, **36-7**, **36-7**, **132-3**
  in Adrianople, 43-9

INDEX

in Alexandria port, 63–6
arrival in 'Akká, 4–6, 7–8, 69–80
   words on arrival in, 77–8
arrival in Haifa, 67
and Badí', 122–3
in Baghdad, 34–6
Bahíyyih Khánum's memories of, 23–31
banished from Adrianople, 50–4
in the barracks, viii, ix, 71–3, 75, 78, 82, 84, 85, 86, 87–9, 91–2, 94, 95–6, 97, 100, 104–6, 107, **132–3**
campaign of Mírzá Yaḥyá against, 46–8
Cause/Faith of, *see* Bahá'í Faith
children of, 10, 21,149
on Constantinople's spiritual condition, 42
correspondence between, and Persian believers, 105
death of Mírzá Mihdí, 144–9, 153–4
   Bahá'u'lláh accepts sacrifice of his life, xiv–xv, 148
declaration of, 15, 40–1, 110
departure from Gallipoli, 54–9
description of, by Professor Browne, 44
description of Ḥaydar-'Alí, Mírzá, 44–6
epistles to kings and rulers, 46, 123, 124
exile of, 15
   compared to those of other Manifestations, 68
family of, *see* Holy Family
hand of, at cell window, ix, 96, 117, 121, **132–3**, 135, 137, 189
healing prayer revealed in barracks, 91–2
home of, in Tehran, 10, 22, 32
journey to Adrianople, 43
journey to 'Akká, 54–5, 57–68
journey to Constantinople, 41
Lawḥ-i-Ra'ís (Tablet to the Chief), 88–9
life in the barracks, 85, 88–9, 90, 100, 138

a Manifestation of God, 125
meets Governor after death of Mírzá Mihdí, 153–4
moved from prison after death of Mírzá Mihdí, 8, 128, 153–5, 202
poem in praise of, 115
poisoned by Mírzá Yaḥyá, 46–7
prophecies of His coming to 'Akká, 2–5, 48, 49, 76–7, 79
prophesies opening of prison doors, 107
relationship with Holy Family, 109–10
and Shaykh Maḥmúd, 76–7, 125–7
Shrine of, 160, 182
in Síyáh-Chál, 11, 24
suffering of, 17, 23, 29, 33, 37, 111, 143, 156–7
in Sulaymáníyyih, 15, 143
summons of, to kings and rulers, 46
Súriy-i-Ra'ís, 190
Tablet for Abu'l-Ḥasan-i-Ardikání, 119
Tablets and prayers of, 167–9, 198, 202
   on death of Mírzá Mihdí, **iv**, viii, 156–9, 166
   on death of Navváb, 172–5
Tablets revealed in the barracks, 107
Bahíyyih Khánum, viii, **36–7**, 8, 10, 21
   on Bahá'u'lláh's meeting with Governor, 153–4
   and death of Mírzá Mihdí, 145, 149–50
   on family relationships, 109–10
   on life in Baghdad, 33–5
   memories of:
      arrival in 'Akká, 70, 71, 72, 73, 78
      arrival in Haifa, 67
      Gallipoli, 54–5, 59
      journey to 'Akká, 50–5, 59, 62, 63, 66
      life in the barracks, 82–5, 90, 92–6, 97

life in Tehran, 23–31
Mírzá Mihdí, 11
Navváb, 11, 21–31, 33–6, 149–50
passing of, 169
resting place of, and monument to, ix, **180–1**, 210, 218, 220
wish that mother and brother be reintered on Mount Carmel, 170–7
Bahíyyih Khánum Fund for Mashriqu'l-Adhkár, 177–8
Bahjí, 210
Baker, Effie, 145
Balyuzi, Hasan M., 16, 188
barracks, 'Akká, viii, ix, 140, 188, 192, 203
  Bahá'u'lláh moved from, as needed for soldiers, 8, 128, 153–5, 202
  Colonel AhmadiJarráh, commander of, 125
  condition of Bahá'í prisoners, 114–16
  conditions in, 90–6, 103–4, 106, 107–9, 114–16, 117
  description of, 87–8, 192
  exiles immediately imprisoned in, 8, 67, 71–3, 75, 81–3, 108, 141, 213
  governor's inspection of, 86
  Hands of the Cause and the Universal House of Justice gather at, 160
  healing prayer revealed in, 91–2
  life in, 81–112
  pilgrims to, 110, 182, 207–8
    see also pilgrims
  renovation of, 192–3, 208
  roof and skylight, ix, xii, xiv, 7, 87, 88, 101–2, 141–5, **132–3**, 164, 187–8, 189, 192–3, 213
  suffering of exiles in, 8, 43, 67, 71–3, 75, 81–7, 101, 108, 141, 142, 208, 213
  water in, 7, 83–4, 85, 93, 103, 151
  see also Most Great Prison
Bayán, the, 116
Beirut, 117, 133
Beveridge, Kent, 59

Blessed Perfection, see Bahá'u'lláh
Boutros, Dr, 95, 124
Branches, 15
British Mandate, 188–9
Browne, Professor Edward Granville, 44

calligraphy, 16–17, 97, 104
Carmel, Mount, 1, 5, 78, 116, 160, 166
  Bahá'ís making their homes on, 121, 130
  Bahá'u'lláh at, 5
  Mírzá Mihdí interred on, 176–82, 209–20
  prophecies concerning, 3
  see also Haifa
Carmel, Tablet of, 179, 180, 181, 203
Chupán, Dr, 47
citadel, see Most Great Prison and barracks, 'Akká
Constantine, (Alexandria) 64–5
Constantinople/Istanbul, viii, **36–7**, 41–2
  exile to, 7, 33, 39–40, 196
  expulsion from, 43
  journey to, 41
contentment, 39
Covenant-breakers, 46, 120–1, 172, 177, 216
Cyprus, 59, 61, 69–70

David, the psalmist, 2

earth tremor, 152, 163
edicts exiling Bahá'u'lláh, 4, 8, 17, 39–40, 48, 51, 54, 55, 67, 69, 108, 138
Edirne, see Adrianople
Ezekiel, 3

Faizi, Abu'l-Qasim, 58, 60, 77–8
Faraj, Áqá, 134
Fáris (Alexandria), 64–5
Fátimih, daughter of 'Alí-'Askar, 91

Gallipoli, viii, 54–5, 190
  journey from, to 'Akká, 57–68, 84
  spiritual significance of, 67–8
Garden of Ridván, 15, 40–1, 195

INDEX

Ghuṣn-i-Aṭhar (the Purest Branch), see Mihdí, Mírzá
Guardian of the Baháʼí Faith, see Shoghi Effendi
guards, 41, 52, 72, 84, 86, 89, 96, 98, 106, 124, 125, 126, 137, 152, 207

Haifa, viii, 121, 123, 175, 182, 203
  arrival of exiles in, 7, 67, 69–70
  Baháʼís in, 130, 135
  fall of, 191
  pilgrimage to, 218
  separation of exiles at Haifa, 60–1
  steamers travelling to, 59
  travel of exiles from Alexandria to, 66–7
  see also Carmel, Mount
Hajj, 117
Haney, Paul, 160
Ḥarám-i-Aqdas, 160
Ḥaydar-ʻAlí, Mírzá, 44–6
Hegira, 68
Heroic Age, 179
Holy Family, viii, ix, **36–7**, 145, **132–3**, 181, 199, 211–12
  Adrianople, 43, 46, 48, 51–3
  journey from, to ʻAkká, 50–5, 57–68
  in ʻAkká, 35, 39, 72, 154, 165–71, 202
  arrival in ʻAkká, 71–2, 78
  in Baghdad, 11, 39–40
  Baháʼuʼlláhʼs declaration of His mission to, 40–1
  condemned to banishment and life imprisonment, 4, 29, 33, 48–9, 54–5, 196
  in Constantinople, 41, 43
  Mírzá Mihdíʼs separation and reunion with, 11–14, 81
  in the Most Great Prison, 8, 81–5, 88, 108–9, 113, 139, 152, 192
  and passing of Mírzá Mihdí, 148–50, 165, 199
  and pilgrims, 130, 136
  relationship among members, 109–10
  reverence of, 109–10
  suffering of, 8, 43, 71, 81–7, 101, 142, 208

  in Tehran, 10–11, 22–30
Hujjat, 32
humanity, unification of, xv, 147, 157, 158, 160, 161, 194, 197, 214–15
Ḥusayn, Mullá, 32
Ḥusayn-Áqá, 91
Ḥusayn-i-Ashchí, 76, 102, 127–9
  on death of Mírzá Mihdí, 145

International Archives Building, 166, 172
Iran, 4, 196
  Baháʼís in, 110, 113, 117, 203
Ismáʻíl, Mírzá, of Yalrúd, 19
Ismáʻíl, Ustád, of Káshán, 130–1, 135
Israel, state of, 1, 192, 196, 207, 208
Istanbul, see Constantinople/Istanbul

Jacob, 143, 187
Jaʻfar, Mírzá, 106–7, 147
Jaffa, 66–7
Jesus, xv, 13, 68, 157, 197, 198, 218
Jews, 3, 188, 192
Job, 143, 187
Julius Caesar, 140

Ketaphakou, Cesar, 124
Khalíl Aḥmad ʻAbdú, 75–6
Kitáb-i-Aqdas, 9

land gate (city gate), ʻAkká, 7, 94, 113, 121, 152, 162, 184
laughter, 107–9
Lawḥ-i-Raʼís (Tablet to the Chief), 88–9
Leaves, 15

Maʻani, Baharieh Rouhani, 151–2, 197–8
Maḥmúd, Shaykh, 76–7, 125–7, 151
Maimonides, 140
Manifestation of God, 116, 148
  see also Baháʼuʼlláh
Marco Polo, 140
Mary and Joseph, 68
Mashhadí Fattáḥ, 91
Mashriquʼl-Adhkár, 178, 180, 181
the Master, see ʻAbduʼl-Bahá

MÍRZÁ MIHDÍ

Mihdí, Mírzá, **iii**, viii, ix, 21, **36–7**
  amanuensis to Bahá'u'lláh, 14–15, 16–17, 96–7, 104, 142, 178, 195, 203, 212
  arrival in 'Akká, 69–80
  attains presence of Bahá'u'lláh, 141
  in Baghdad, 11–12, 14, 36, 39
  in the barracks, 81–112
  calligraphy of, 16–17, 97
  centenary of his death, 159–61
  childhood of, 10–18
  death of, 8, 18, 139–55, 204, 213–15
    Bahá'u'lláh moved from prison afterwards, 8, 128, 153–5, 202
    circumstances of, 142–4
    falls through skylight, xiv, 144, 213
    funeral of, 151–3, 162–3, 197, 215
    wishes that his life may be sacrificed, 148, 214
  delicate constitution, 31, 81, 114, 194, 211
  descriptions of, 15–16, 194–5, 200–1, 205, 212
  educated by his mother and Mírzá Músá, 15, 105
  life of, inspires youth, ix, 196–7, 201–4
  a life of spiritual meaning, 197
  life without him, 162–75
  monument to, 160, 178, **180–1**
  naming of, 10–11
  pebbles/stones of, 166, 183–4, 197
  a 'ransom', 18, 147, 149, 159–60, 178, 201, 215
  reinterment on Mount Carmel, 176–82, 209–20
  roof and skylight of barracks, ix, xii, xiv, 7, 87, 88, 101–2, 141–5, **132–3**, 164, 187–8, 189, 192–3, 213
  sacrifice, meaning and effect of Mírzá Mihdí's, ix, xiii–xv, 138, 145, 152–3, 156–61, 182, 197–9, 202, 214–15
    that doors to prison might open, xiv, 138, 154
  sends sweets to Nabíl from ship in Alexandria, 65, 195
  separation from and reunion with parents, 11–14, 81
  service, 111, 196, 201–2, 204
  spiritual qualities of, 15
  suffering of, 11, 81–7, 101, 144, 146, 148, 150, 156–7, 166, 187, 197, 212–13
  Tablet of Bahá'u'lláh on death of, 156–7
  titled 'The Purest Branch' (Ghuṣn-i-Aṭhar), 15, 187, 194–5
  the 'trust of God and His treasure', 153, 156, 200–1
Momen, Moojan, xii, xiii–xv, 116–17
Moses, 20, 68, 69
Most Great House, 36–8
Most Great Prison (Citadel), viii, ix, 1–9, 33, **36–7**, 68, 77, 119, 124, **132–3**, 131, 139, 156, 159, 162, 181, 182, 214
  Bahá'ís who passed away in, 16
  Bahá'u'lláh's description of, 17
  Bahá'u'lláh prophesies opening of prison doors, 107
  condition of Bahá'í prisoners, 114–16
  conditions in, relaxed, 153, description of, by a pilgrim, 189
  Mírzá Mihdí's death, *see* Mihdí, Mírzá
  pilgrims to, 110, 113–38
  prison conditions, 90–1, 106, 107–9, 114–16, 117
  so designated by Bahá'u'lláh, 9
  see also barracks, 'Akká
Mosul, 117, 130, 132, 134
Mount Carmel, *see* Carmel, Mount
Muhammad, Prophet, 15, 68, 77, 198
Muḥammad-'Alí, 35
Muḥammad-Báqir, Áqá, 88, 154
Muḥammad-Ismá'il, Áqá, 88, 154
Muḥammad-Qulí, Mírzá, 88
Muníb, Jináb-i-, 61–2
Munírih Khánum, 177, 181
Músá, Mírzá (Áqáy-i-Kalím), 24, 26, 28, 35, 47, 88, 105
music, 99
Mytilene (Madellí), 61

INDEX

Nabí Ṣáliḥ cemetery, ix, 152, **132-3**, 162, 163, 175, 211
Nabíl-i-Aẓam, 32, 50, 146-7
  enters citadel, 121-2
  sends a message to Bahá'u'lláh on His ship in Alexandria, 63-5
  unable to see Bahá'u'lláh in 'Akká, 120-2, 135, 136
Nabíl-i-Qá'iní, 129, 135, 163
Najib Pasha, 40
Napoleon, 1-2, 140
Napoleon III, 124
Náṣiri'd-Dín Sháh, *see* Shah of Iran
Navváb (Ásíyih Khánum, the Most Exalted Leaf), ix,18-22, 33, 158-9,
  in 'Akká, 93, 94
  and arrest of Bahá'u'lláh, 22-6
  Bahíyyih Khánum's memories of, 11, 21-31, 33-6
  in the barracks, 103
  children of, 10, 21,149
  and death of Mírzá Mihdí, 144-7, 149-50, 152, 164-7, 169
  descriptions of, 19-20, 21
  education of her children, 15, 105
  grandchildren of, 169
  home of, 10, 22, 32
  marriage of, 20-1
  monument to, ix, 160, 178, **180-1**
  passing of, ix, 170-5
  reinterment on Mount Carmel, 176-82, 209-20
  Shoghi Effendi's description of, 19, 171-2
  suffering of, 24, 144, 146-7, 149-50, 166, 171-2
  Tablets of Bahá'u'lláh in honour of, 172-5
  and Ṭáhirih, 32
  Ṭúbá Khánum's memories of, 103-4, 169-71
Neugeboren, Jay, 199
Noah, 143, 187
Núr, 10

Ode of the Dove (Qaṣídiy-i-Varqá'íyyih), 143-4, 184-7
An Orphan's Tale (Neugeboren), 199
Ottomans, viii, 4, 7, 46, 75, 88, 93, 153, 192, 203
  collapse of Empire, 188, 190

Passengers on the Deck of a Steam Packet in the Adriatic Sea, viii, xii, xiii, **36-7**
Paul, St, 140
pebbles/stones, of Mírzá Mihdí, 166, 183-4, 197
persecution, following attempt on the life of the Shah, 22-30
Phelps, Myron, 100-1
pilgrims, 160, 166, 169, 182, 189-90, 193, 207-8
  to Adrianople, 46
  to 'Akká, ix, xiv, 110, 113-38
  doors open for, to visit Bahá'u'lláh, xiv, 154-5, 162, 182
  glimpse Bahá'u'lláh's hand at cell window, ix, 96, 117, 121, **132-3**, 135, 137, 189
  route taken by, 117
Pius IX, Pope, 124
poem, in praise of Bahá'u'lláh, 115
Port Said, 66
prison, *see* barracks, 'Akká and Most Great Prison
Promised One, *see* Bahá'u'lláh
prophecies, of Bahá'u'lláh coming to, 2-5, 48, 49, 76-7, 79
Purest Branch (Ghuṣn-i-Aṭhar), *see* Mihdí, Mírzá
purity, xiv, 194-5, 206, 210

Qaṣídiy-i-Ṭá'íyyih (Ibn-i-Fárid), 185
Qazvin, 156-7
Qiblih, 180, 210
Quddús, 32

Richardson, Henry Burdon, viii, xii
Riḍá, Áqá, 16, 58-9
Riḍván (holy day), 100
Ruhe, David, 153
Russia/Russian Consul, 27-9, 55, 153, 203

sacrifice, meaning and effect of Mírzá Mihdí's, ix, xiii-xv, 138, 145, 152-3, 156-61, 182, 197-9, 202, 214-15

Salmán, Shaykh, 104–5
Sárih Khánum, 12
Saturno, 59
sea gate, 'Akká, viii, 8, **36–7**, 69, 71, 73, 79–80
Shah of Iran (Násiri'd-Dín Sháh), viii, 3, 19, 23, **36–7**, 33, 40
  attempt on the life of, 28
  letter of Bahá'u'lláh to, 123
Shíshmán, 47
Shoghi Effendi, 3
  on 'Akká, 6–7
  on Bahá'u'lláh's arrival in 'Akká, 70
  on Bahá'u'lláh's banishment to 'Akká, 49
  contribution to Bahíyyih Khánum Fund for Mashriqu'l-Adhkár, 177–8
  on departure of exiles from Gallipoli, 57
  gives Bahá'u'lláh's shirt to Iraq, 146
  on history of Bahá'í Faith, xiii
  on Navváb, 19, 171–2
  on Ode of the Dove, 185–6
  on passing of Mírzá Mihdí, 152, 188
  on poisoning of Bahá'u'lláh, 46–7
  reinters Mírzá Mihdí and Navváb on Mount Carmel, 175, 176–82, 209–20
  on response of Iranian Bahá'ís to imprisonment of Bahá'u'lláh, 113
  on sacrifice of Mírzá Mihdí, 157–8
  on service to the Cause, 201
  student at Oxford, 204
  on Ustád Ismá'íl, 130
Shrine of Bahá'u'lláh, 160, 182
Siyáh-Chál, 11, 24
Smyrna, 60, 61–2
'The Spiritual Potencies of that Consecrated Spot', 178–80
steamers/steamships, viii, xii, 41, 55, 56–7, 59, 60, 62, 66–7, 69, 134, 184
stones/pebbles, of Mírzá Mihdí, 166, 183–4, 197

stories, funny, 107–9
Suez Canal, 56, 66
Sulaymáníyyih, 15, 143
Sultan of Turkey/Ottomans, *see* 'Abdu'l-Azíz, Sultan
Sultán, Shaykh, 35
Sultanate, abolished, 189

Ṭabarsí, siege at, 32
Tablet of Visitation, 160, 218
Taherzadeh, Adib, 75–6, 100, 104, 136–7, 158, 186, 188, 202
Ṭáhirih, 32, 34, 35, 194–5
Tehran, viii, 11, 13, 19–31, **36–7**, 123, 185
  Bahá'u'lláh exiled from, 14, 29
  Bahá'u'lláh's house in, 10
  Bahíyyih Khánum's memories of life in, 23–31
  Mírzá Mihdí remains in, 11–14, 81, 185
Ṭúbá Khánum, 103–4, 169–71
Tudor Pole, Wellesley, 190–1
Turkish prime minister ('Alí Páshá), 88, 124, 190

Údí Khammár, house of, 165
UNESCO World Heritage Site, 80
the Universal House of Justice, xi, 67–8, 159–61, 180, 200, 203, 204, 207
'Uthmán Effendi, 125

Vaḥíd, 32
Victoria, Queen, 124

water, 6–7, 39, 43, 48, 63, 83–5, 93, 103, 207
World Centre, 160, 172

Yaḥyá, Mírzá, 46, 48, 59, 60–1, 69–70, 113, 120
  poisons Bahá'u'lláh, 47
  poisons of well of Holy Family, 48
youth, ix, 101, 103, 122, 152, 156, 160–1, 178, 196–7, 199–204, 211, 212, 213, 214

www.ingramcontent.com/pod-product-compliance
Lightning Source LLC
Chambersburg PA
CBHW060113170426
43198CB00010B/877